The Rulers of Russia and the Russian Farmers

By Rev. Denis Fahey, C.S.SP., D.D., D.PH., B.A.

Professor of Philosophy and Church History, Holy Ghost Missionary College,
Kimmage, Dublin

"In the beginning Communism showed itself for what it was in all its perversity; but very soon it realized that it was alienating the people. It has therefore changed its tactics, and strives to entice the multitudes by trickery of various forms, hiding its real designs. . ... Without receding an inch from their subversive principles, Communists invite Catholics to collaborate with them in the realm of humanitarianism and charity. . ... Elsewhere they carry their hypocrisy so far as to encourage the belief that Communism . . . will not interfere with the practice of religion. . ... See to it, Venerable Brethren, that the faithful do not allow themselves to be deceived! Communism is intrinsically wrong"

"Those who permit themselves to be deceived into lending their aid towards the triumph of Communism in their own country will be the first to fall victims of their error. And the greater the antiquity and grandeur of the Christian civilization in the regions where Communism successfully penetrates, so much the more devastating will be the hatred displayed by the Godless."

Encyclical Letter of Pope Pius XI,
Divini Redemptoris, *on Atheistic Communism*

IMPRIMI POTEST: P. O'Carroll, C. S. Sp.,

Praep. Prov. Hib.

NIHIL OBSTAT: Thomas Morris S.T.D.,

Censor Deputatus.

IMPRIMATUR: Jeremias,

† *Archiepiscopus Cassiliensis*
22a *Aprillis*, 1948

First Printed September, 1948
First Loreto Printing October, 2010
ISBN: 1-930278-93-4

All Rights Reserved
Loreto Publications
P. O. Box 603 Fitzwilliam, NH 03447
www.loretopubs.org • Tele: 603.239.6671

Dedication

To the Immaculate Heart of our Blessed Mother, Mediatrix of all Graces; to St. Joseph, Protector of the Universal Church; to St. Michael and the Angel Guardians of all countries, this book is humbly and lovingly dedicated by the author.

Acknowledgments

The author begs to return grateful thanks to the following publishers, who have kindly allowed him to quote from books published by them: Mesgrs. Sheed and Ward, for *Shaw George Versus Bernard*, by J. P. Hackett; The Macmillan Company, Publishers, 65th Avenue, New York, for *Collectivism: A False Utopia*, by William Henry Chamberlin; Human Events Associates, Chicago, U.S.A., for *Blueprint for World Conquest*; George G. Harrap & Company, Ltd., London, for *Assignment in Utopia*, by Eugene Lyons; The Yale University Press; U.S.A., for *The Real Soviet Russia*, by David J. Dallin; Robert Hale, Ltd., London, for *I Chose Freedom*, by Victor Kravchenko, and *I Was a Soviet Worker*, by Andrew Smith; John S. Burns and Sons, Glasgow, for *Twenty Questions about Russia*, by H. W. Henderson, and Faber and Faber Limited, for *The Dark Side of the Moon*.

Contents

Loreto's Introduction to Father Denis Fahey 7
Editor's Notes 11
Biographical Sketch of Father Fahey 12

Chapter One:
Marx's Program for the world 13

Chapter Two:
Lenin and Collectivism 19

Chapter Three:
Stalin Renews the War on the Russian Farmers. 23

Chapter Four:
First Result of Collectivization: Famine 35

Chapter Five:
Second Result of Collectivization:
Enormous Crop of Officials 45

Chapter Six:
Third Result of Collectivization: No Increase in
Production in Spite of Enormous Expense 49

Chapter Eight:
G. B. Shaw, Philosopher and Enemy
of Private Property. 59

Chapter Nine:
Another Innocent Abroad 69

Loreto's Introduction to Father Denis Fahey

When Jesus Christ, our King and Master, taught us how to pray to His Father and Our Father, he used the phrase "thy kingdom come, thy will be done, on *earth* as it is in heaven." In heaven God's will is perfectly accomplished, but here on earth, fallen mankind cannot fulfill God's will without the constant assistance of sanctifying grace communicated to the world through the sacraments of His church.

After the fall of Adam, a world perfectly ordered to God's divine will was corrupted and **dis**-order became the 'natural' state of mankind and the created universe. It was the role of the Messias to **re**-order this fallen world—to bring a new state of order to the world His Father had created. The means for establishing that order by which a fallen world may return to God is the Catholic church and the life of sanctifying grace. As Christians newly born into the life of grace—a 'supernatural' state of being—we are all called to bring as much order to this world as is possible, all the while never forgetting that this world is in a fallen and corrupted state and that a 'utopia' is not possible here on earth. The Church of Christ is constantly opposed in this mission by all of the forces of 'naturalism' or **dis**-order, that is those forces opposed to the supernatural life of divine grace. It is the duty of all Christians of the Church Militant to battle against these forces.

This calling of Christians to the battle for order was the motto of the pontificate of Pope Saint X. That motto was *Instaurare Omnia in Christo,* "to restore all things in Christ", taken from Saint Paul's letter to the Ephesians 1:10. The modern popes have frequently warned us of the dangers of 'naturalism', which denies the supernatural life of grace and militates against it, and they have called us to fight in our private and public lives against this pernicious error. No priest has heeded that call and risen to defend the supernatural life of grace as clearly and as vigorously as Father Denis Fahey. He truly understood, and explained why, there is no salvation outside the Catholic church, either for individual persons or for the life of <u>society</u> and of <u>nations</u>.

A clear image of just what the life of a Christian *in a society imbued from top to bottom with the social principles of Christ the King* would be like, is not a widely shared understanding in much of the Christian world today, especially in America. We must remember that Christianity is a religion of world conquest! We are called to conquer the world for Christ and to do all that we can to subdue persons and nations to His will. A Catholic undertakes this battle first within himself and then within his family. Soon the influence of many families begins to pervade the community and then the nation or state. If Christian people do not have the full picture in their mind of exactly what God's Plan for Order in this world would look like in its accomplishment, then they can have no long-term strategy for victory and little hope of achieving it. We have all of the tools required and all of the powers of heaven backing us. Let us take into our hearts and our minds the full plan and its potential for the realization of peace in the world and Christ the King of heaven and earth will bless our efforts. This was the permanent admonition of Fr. Fahey.

Father Fahey was a seminarian and was ordained in Rome during the pontificate of Pius X. The young priest was deeply influenced and inspired by that pope. When he penned a short *Apologia* for his work, Father Fahey expressed his vocation in this fashion:

> "When in Rome I began to realize more fully the real significance of the history of the world, as the account of the acceptance and rejection of Our Lord's Program for Order. I used to ask permission to remain at the Confession of St. Peter, while the other scholastics went round the basilica.
>
> "I spent the time there going over the history of the world, and I repeatedly promised Saint Peter that if I ever got the chance, I would teach the truth about his Master in the way he and his successors, the Roman Pontiffs, wanted it done.
>
> That is what I have striven to do and am doing."

Father Fahey not only clarified, explained, taught, and defended 'Our Lord's Program for Order' in the world, he also actively fought and exposed the persons who were the enemies of that order. Because he did so, he has often been called 'negative' or 'anti-Semitic', or 'much too concerned with Masonic conspiracies'. These are the pathetic terms of opprobrium hurled with such energy by those enemies of Christ whose plans he has effectively opposed. But in this he was in good company with St. Louis Marie de Montfort and Our Lady, who appears 'terrible as an army set in battle array' to the enemies of her divine son.

Listen to the words of St. Louis Marie as he stresses the two functions of our Blessed Mother, the *positive* one of making Our Lord known, and the negative one of making war upon His enemies.

> Mary must be manifested more than ever by her mercy, her power and her grace in these latter times; by her mercy, bringing back and lovingly welcoming the poor strayed sinners who will be converted and will return to the Catholic Church; by her power, against the enemies of God, idolaters, schismatics, Mohammedans, Jews, and men hardened in impiety, who will rise in terrible revolt to seduce all those who oppose them and to make them fall by promises and threats; she must also be made manifest by her grace animating and sustaining the valiant soldiers and faithful servants of Jesus Christ, who shall battle for His interests.
>
> And lastly, Mary must be terrible to the devil and his ministers, as an army in battle array, principally in these latter times, because the devil knowing that he has but little time, and now less than ever, to damn souls, will every day redouble his efforts and his combats. He will before long raise up cruel persecutions and will lay terrible snares for the faithful servants and true children of Mary whom he finds more difficult to conquer than the others.

Loreto Publications is committed to re-issuing all of the previously published works of Fr. Fahey and making them available to a much wider audience. The works of Fr. Fahey are critically important for Catholics to read, understand, and disseminate in our day when the forces of 'organized naturalism' or 'anti-supernaturalism' seem to be rampaging triumphantly through the Church and the world today. Arm yourselves for the battle!

Loreto Publications intends to publish the following works of Fr. Denis Fahey:

Mental Prayer According to the Teaching of Saint Thomas Aquinas (1927)
The Kingship of Christ According to the Principles of Saint Thomas Aquinas (1931)
The Mystical Body of Christ in the Modern World (1935)
* *The Rulers of Russia* (1938)
* *The Workingmen's Guilds of the Middle Ages* (1943)
    (A translation of the work by Dr. Godefroid Kurth C.S.G.)
The Kingship of Christ and Organized Naturalism (1943)
* *Money Manipulation and the Social Order* (1944)
The Mystical Body of Christ (1945)
The Mystical Body of Christ and the Reorganization of Society (1945)
* *The Tragedy of James Connolly* (1947)
* *The Rulers of Russia and the Russian Farmers* (1948)
The Kingship of Christ and the Conversion of the Jewish Nation (1953)
The Church and Farming (1953)
The Duties of the Catholic State in Regard to Religion (1954)
    (A translation of the work by Cardinal Alfredo Ottaviani)

* Currently available from Loreto

Editor's notes

Loreto's editions of the works of Father Fahey have been newly typeset and updated with some changes to the original text. The alterations are as follows:

1. We have changed the spelling of many words to match modern American spelling rules. Some examples are: neighbor for neighbour, show for shew, labor for labour, realize for realise, mold for mould, program for programme, etc.

2. We have made use of current punctuation and capitalization rubrics.. 3. We have made a few minor corrections of typographical errors in the original texts but have NOT altered the words of Fr. Fahey nor made any deletions.

4. We have made uniform the notations of scripture references in the currently accepted fashion. For example, we use Mt. 24: 6–9 instead of Matt. xxiv 6, 7, 8, 9.

Biographical sketch of Father Denis Fahey, C.S.Sp.

(July 3, 1883 – January 21, 1954)

Denis Fahey was born in Golden, County Tipperary, Ireland, on the land and among kinsmen whom he dearly loved. The parish of Knockavilla where he was baptized is part of the Diocese of Cashel. He was, by the grace of God born into a devout Catholic family that was blessed with three sons. Thomas was the oldest. John died very young, and Denis was the youngest son of his parents, Thomas and Brigit (Cleary), who were deeply devoted to the Church. Denis was sent at the age of twelve to Rockwell College, where he was educated by the Holy Ghost Fathers among whom his vocation to the priesthood was nurtured and eventually came to fruition.

At the age of 17 he entered the novitiate of the Holy Ghost Fathers at Grignon-Orly, near Paris. He made his religious profession on February 2, 1907 and was ordained to the priesthood in Rome on September 24, 1910. The ordination was conferred by Cardinal Respighi at St. John Lateran.

Father Fahey's life work was the promotion of the Catholic social doctrine of Christ the King. He firmly believed that "the world must conform to Our Divine Lord, not He to it." He always defended the Mystical Body of Christ without compromise.

"See to it, Venerable Brethren, that the faithful do not allow themselves to be deceived! Communism is intrinsically wrong."

From the encyclical letter of Pope Pius XI, *Divini Redemptoris,* on Atheistic Communism

Chapter One
Marx's Program for the World

OUTLINE OF MARX'S FUNDAMENTAL IDEAS

In order to get a clear idea of life in Russia as it really is and of the sort of organization of agriculture which those who wield power there are preparing for the world, we must return to the ideas inspiring those rulers. They need to be strongly emphasized, because writers of articles in newspapers and even of books about Russia rarely point out the background of ideas which all the rulers of Russia are seeking to realize. All the tactical maneuvers of those rulers are directed towards the realization of those ideas. There have been, and are struggles between them, but the struggles are concerned with the best strategic moves to make in order to realize a certain program. The ideas in the program are always the same, namely, those of Karl Marx (family name, Mardochai), with their logical consequences.

Let us first give an outline of Marx's fundamental ideas. Marx (1818-1883) holds that all that is in the world is evolving matter. This is derived from Feuerbach (1804-1872) from the point of view of its *materialism*, and from Hegel (1770-1831) from the point of view of its *method* of explaining the evolution of the world. In Hegel's system, a thesis (assertion or affirmation) gives rise to an antithesis or contradiction, both of which disappear in the unity of a synthesis. This synthesis becomes in its turn a thesis to which there arises an antithesis and so on. Of course, what is contradiction

13

between ideas or doctrines becomes conflict and war between human beings. For Hegel, therefore, war is not an accident. It is the law of the universe. Marx applied these ideas to the evolution of the world. Human thought is an attribute of material being, of the human body and the brain. The organization of society by human thought is due to the action of the prevailing economic conditions on man's brain development. Men are purely material and are therefore without immortal rational souls, just like other animals. These purely material men in turn modify and change the matter of which future men are composed, by means of changes of the methods of production. By these new methods, the thoughts and attitudes of men towards life are modified, for thought is a product of matter. Thus there is rupture of equilibrium in the existing organization of society by the uprise of the "Hegelian antithesis," leading to a new state of unstable equilibrium. The class war is, therefore, the law of the universe.

This gives us an outline of history down to the time when the world will have attained its ideal equilibrium by the disappearance of warring classes on the establishment of world—Communism. The establishment of the Communist state in Russia ushers in the dawn of that happy era. The state of tension in the capitalist countries is a clear indication of that rupture of equilibrium, which is preparing the way for the conquest of power by the proletariat. The class war must be stirred up and envenomed, in order to accelerate the process and achieve the definitive (Hegelian) synthesis by a worldwide union of Soviet Republics. When men have been liberated from capitalist exploitation, they will become accustomed to observe the rules of social life without force and without subjection. The causes of crimes and excesses will wither away and with their disappearance the state will wither away also. Human beings will become completely unselfish and will sacrifice themselves without effort for the good of the community. There will be another world, in fact, a new era, when human nature will have been suitably molded by Marxian education.

The proletariat class then, according to Marx, is a messianic class destined by its rule to bring about a new era of definitive peace for the world. Here Marx abandons Hegel and Feuerbach, according to whom it would be logical to expect that another rupture of equilibrium or antithesis would supervene, followed by a new synthesis. In the place of logical reasoning he substitutes the messianic traditions of his childhood, for the realization of which the Russian people are simply a means.

THE CENTRAL POINT IN MARX'S PROGRAM

To use the language of St. Thomas Aquinas, every human being is both an individual and a person. On the one hand, owing to his having a material nature like the animals, that is to say, on account of the fact that he is an individual, man is a component part of the whole formed by the family or by civil society. In this respect he is directly ordained to society; he is only indirectly ordained to Gad. On the other hand owing to his having an immaterial soul, by which he resembles the angels, that is to say, owing to his being a person, he is directly ordained to God, and society exists for him. The individual is for society, as the part is for the whole, the hand for the body, but society is for the person.

For Marx and his disciples, Lenin, Trotsky, Stalin and consorts, man is only an individual like all animals, though somewhat more evolved. He is not a human person. The idea that he has an immaterial soul, by which he can enter directly into relation with God, is merely a bourgeois prejudice. Let us now see some of the consequences of this fundamental doctrine.

A. Human Beings are Completely at the Mercy of the Collectivity

According to Marxian Communism, which is the guiding philosophy of the rulers of Russia, a human being is merely an individual completely subject to the collectivity, that is to the group or party that has seized power therein. He is not a person. He is merely an animal. This means that he will be treated like a donkey or a dog or an insect to be moved about, beaten or trodden upon, as those in power think the interests of Marxian evolution demand. He has no personal rights that the state must respect. There is no moral law, natural or revealed, of which the leaders of the Communist party are bound to take account in their dealings with their fellow men. Neither is there any such thing as conscience, as we understand the term.

In his authoritative book, *Problems of Leninism,* Stalin is perfectly in line with Marx when he characterizes the rule of the Communist Party in the U.S.S.R. as rule "based on force" and "unrestricted by law."

B. Private Property Must be Eliminated

For Marxism there is no such thing as personality in our sense with definite inalienable rights. Accordingly, there can be no such thing as the right to own permanently any of the means of production. As human beings are purely material like the animals. All the matter of the world, the soil, the plants and the animals, belong to all men equally and can belong to no one in particular. Men may have things which perish in the use of them just like the animals, but being mere animals, they have not the right to own land and productive goods in stable possession. Human beings are simply brute matter evolving from the earth and returning completely thereto. Accordingly, Marxists hold that private property in the means of production is always exploitation. Human labor, being the labor not of a person, but of an individual, a mere animal belonging completely to the collectivity, creates value for society. Private ownership thus means withholding from society the values created by the labor of an animal belonging completely to society. Marxism, therefore, will always seek to eliminate private ownership. It may have to make tactical concessions and to bide its time, but the aim will always be the same and will dictate action, when the favorable moment will have arrived.

C. No Religion: No Moral Law

An animal cannot have religion. Accordingly, though Marxism may make a truce with religion for a time, for motives of expediency, it can never logically abandon its aim of destroying every vestige of religion. It must combat especially the claim of the Catholic Church, as the sole divinely appointed guardian of the moral law, that that law is binding on states as well as on private persons. Marxian Communism acknowledges no moral law. Logically it cannot do so, as mere animals cannot even know the moral law. People find it hard to believe that the moral law, the Ten Commandments, for, example, have no meaning for Communists. Yet the testimonies of Marx and Lenin are quite clear and unmistakable. "Law, morality, religion," writes Marx in *The Communist Manifesto,* "are to him (the proletariat) so many bourgeois prejudices behind which lurk in ambush so many bourgeois interests." Of course we must link up this with Marx's doctrine outlined at the beginning of this article. The "bourgeois prejudices" of morality and religion were the result of the economic conditions of the past. With a new economic organization these prejudices will disappear.

"We deny all morality in the bourgeois sense," wrote Lenin, "for according to the bourgeois, morality had its origin in the Commandments of God. We affirm that we do not believe in God . . . . Our morality, on the contrary, is entirely subordinate to the interests of the proletariat and to the 'exigencies of the class war' . . . We proclaim moral whatever serves to destroy the old exploiting form of society and to unite together all the workers for the creation of the new Communist society. For us Communists, whatever is useful for this struggle is moral . . . We do not believe in an eternal moral law."[1]

For Communists, therefore, lying is not a sin, when a lie serves to advance what they consider to be the interests of Communism. We shall have to remind our reader of this when we come to consider the account of civilization in Russia given in *Soviet Policy in Agriculture*, published by *The Friends of Soviet Russia*, about 1930. The foreword to the pamphlet states that it "goes thoroughly into the agricultural problem in the Soviet Union and shows how the backward, despised, oppressed peasant, used to starvation, rags, and the most brutal punishments, is growing to the full stature of a free man under Bolshevism. He reaps and enjoys as his inalienable right the harvest that he sows. By the vigor and decisiveness of his fight against the kulak, the robber whom he deprived of the power to rob, he broke resolutely with the 'private property' fetish and opened his mind to Socialism."

---

[1]. Cf. *The Mystical Body of Christ in the Modern World*, p. 230.

Chapter Two:
Lenin and Collectivism

FAMINE FOLLOWS LENIN'S ATTEMPT AT COLLECTIVIZATION

What we may call the opening skirmish in the battle against the Russian farmers took place in 1919-1921. In those years Lenin tried to apply Marxian collectivism, based on the doctrine that man is merely an animal, to the Russian countryside. The peasants resisted the intolerable demands made upon them. They refused to grow food for "the pampered cities and armies." Thus Eugene Lyons expresses it in *Assignment in Utopia* (p. 98). The result was a terrible famine. In his book, *The Fall of the Russian Empire*, Rev. Edmund A. Walsh, S.J., who spent from March (1922) to November (1923) on relief work in Russia, describes the state of the country as follows: "The Russian people, at the moment, were passing through the well-nigh mortal travail of the most appalling famine in their long and stormy history. Twenty-three million human beings were threatened with 'extermination by inevitable starvation', and their cry for help had been answered generously by Europe and America. Six million succumbed, despite the heroic efforts of combined relief agencies, making the valley of the Volga a huge graveyard, and turning the river itself into a charnel house with thousands upon thousands of skeletonized corpses congealed beneath the ice."

Lest anyone may object that this testimony is exaggerated, it is well to add that the twenty months Fr. Walsh spent in Russia were not passed exclusively in Moscow and Petrograd, but—to quote his own words—"in the Crimea and the Ukraine, in the Caucasus and the Black Sea districts, along the Volga and the Sea of Azov, in the Don Cossack country and among the Tartars, in peasant huts and ruined palaces, as well as under the shadow of the Kremlin. The territory covered stretched from the Gulf of Finland to the Kuban, and from the Carpathians to the foothills of the Ural mountains."

Pope Pius XI refers to this period in his Letter, *The Soviet Campaign Against God* (2nd February, 1930): "The generous offerings of the Catholic world saved from famine and a horrible death, more than 150,000 children, who were daily fed by our envoys, until they were forced to abandon their pious work by those who preferred to give thousands of innocent children to death rather than see them fed by Christian charity." In the later famine of 1932–1933, Stalin did not permit an appeal to the charity of the world, as Lenin had done. We may conclude from this that Marx's teaching, according to which human beings do not count in the process of preparing the messianic era, was better grasped as time went on. "If twenty millions die of hunger," said the Communist Party Secretary to Andrew Smith, at a Party meeting in 1933, "we will still have plenty of people to continue our work. And what does it matter if millions of people die, so long as we are building Socialism!" Here was a Communist leader cold-bloodedly defending the systematic starvation of an entire people and actually justifying the wiping out of millions . . .. Who would be left to enjoy the Socialist paradise of the future, if human beings were allowed to die by millions in the meantime?"[1]

An Uneasy Truce

"Lenin", as Father Walsh says, "died the thousand living deaths of a deranged paralytic before his actual demise in 1924," but he had the sense to see in 1922 that the principles of Karl Marx could not yet be pushed to their final savage conclusions. He compromised. The introduction of the N.E.P. (New Economic Policy), permitting private trade brought about

---

[1] *I Was a Soviet Worker*, (p. 196). This is a good study by a Communist, disillusioned by a three years sojourn in Russia as a factory worker.

an uneasy peace. A certain revival of agriculture took place, though the majority of the farmers feared a renewed application of Marx's principles. Having restored their economy "more or less to the pre-war level, they had acquired a modest measure of security . . . . To have gone beyond that would have meant rising from the status of Seredniaki—middle peasants—to that of kulaks and exposing themselves to possible reprisals in the event of a political shift. In many places the peasants feared to sow too much, or to increase the number of their cattle; they purposely divided their land among their children, in order not to be thought to have too much property. In this way the number of peasant households artificially increased from 16,000,000 at the beginning of the revolution to 25,000,000 in the middle twenties . . .. The area of grain cultivation, which had fallen from 232 million acres in 1913 to 162 million in 1922, rose speedily under the N.E.P. to 232 million in 1926. At that point, however, it remained stationary."[2]

The threat to the development of life in the countryside, contained in the principles of Karl Marx, was there all the time. The pamphlet, *Soviet Policy in Agriculture,*" is quite correct in stating that, "the institution of the N.E.P. was not only a strategic operation to re-establish the free market, to give certain possibilities to free commerce. It was above all a grand maneuver to allow of the preparation of a new decisive offensive against the capitalist elements of both town and country."

[2.] *The Real Soviet Russia*, by David J. Dallin, p. 167. This work, published by the Yale University Press, is an excellently documented study of Soviet Russia, showing the results of Marx's philosophy in practice. A little further on, I shall have to point out the rejection of the Divine Plan for Order of the True Supernatural Messias, our Lord Jesus Christ, in Eugene Lyons' book *Assignment in Utopia*. The same rejection is to be found implicitly in D. J. Dallin's book on page 55, where there is an allusion to the "vague ideology" of Catholicism and the Mass. It may be remarked in passing that the French quotation there given is not accurate. D. J. Dallin's rejection of the program of Christ the King is deeply to be regretted, but his work is a very fine general study of the political and economic organization of the Soviet Union. An edition has recently been published in England by Hollis and Carter.

Chapter Three:
Stalin Renews the War on the Russian Farmers

STALIN AND TROTSKY

As the collectivity owns everything and human beings are only animals, those who exercise power in a Marxian state must logically strive to realize complete collectivization of farms. Besides, they want to reduce all to the same dependence on the state as the industrial workers in towns. Trotsky wanted to apply the principles of Marx to the countryside in 1926–27. Stalin insisted that the scheme of collectivization, which he ushered in in 1928–29, would have been premature in 1926–27. If Trotsky had got his program adopted in 1927, he would have been just as ruthless in its application as Stalin was to be later. The quarrel between Trotsky and Stalin was not about the treatment of human beings as mere animals. They were in agreement on that point.

THE OPENING OF THE CAMPAIGN

We can pass lightly over the greater part of 1929. Thousands of descendants of German settlers on the Lower Volga arrived in Moscow in the autumn of 1929 in a desperate attempt to get to Canada. This "episode," writes Eugene Lyons in *Assignment in Utopia* (p. 274), "shook many foreign observers out of their complacency. It gave them a glimpse of the terror that had already gripped the nation's peasantry. We had become inured to newspaper and private accounts of murder, mass arrests and indiscriminate executions that year . . . . As pressure in the villages increased, tens of thousands flocked to the cities. Moscow railroad stations began to look like encampments. Additional border guards and bloodhounds were placed along the Western frontier to stop the wild scramble of frightened peasants from Russia into Romania, Poland and the Baltic countries.

Stringent orders were issued to local Soviets and railroad functionaries to prevent the flight of peasants . . . . My dispatches during these months spoke of the remarkable "success" of the collectivization policies . . . . It was an open secret that these "successes" were based on naked force. Repeatedly, the same weapon had been used against the peasants. Each time the government had been obliged to retreat . . . . This time there would be no retreat."[1] How different is this picture, outlined by an observer in Russia, from that which is painted to us in the Communist pamphlet, *Soviet Policy in Agriculture*. In this publication we read: "The progress in collectivization has

---

[1.] Eugene Lyons, an American-Jewish journalist, deeply in sympathy with Communism, spent six years in Russia from 1928 to 1934. He left it a saddened and disillusioned man. Yet he speaks of the word "revolution" as hallowed by "what happened in France in 1789 and in Russia in 1917." He evidently thinks that Marxian materialism and Communism can be installed without the degradation of the human person and the complete violation of the moral law. This is absolutely absurd. He even talks of "the fascist attack on the democratic government in Spain," as if the so-called democratic government of Spain were not a government of the same savages that he had seen at work in Moscow. On the other hand he sees "the decadence of the moral sense of mankind," as he expresses it. But, alas, in common with his nation, he rejects the Divine Plan for Order in the world through the Mystical Body of Christ, and he does not see what Pope Pius XII insists upon, namely, that "the reeducation, the remolding of the human race . . . must spring from the doctrine of a Divine Redeemer as its only possible fountain source (Encyclical Letter, *Summi Pontificatus*). The moral and ethical values, whose repudiation Eugene Lyons deplores, and the respect of the human person, can be restored only by the return to the full acceptance of the program of Christ the King. There is no other way.

been phenomenal, . . . In six weeks ten million individual peasant families took the decisive step towards Socialism, thus replying to the capitalists of the whole world, who can only maintain their power by repression and fascist terror over the workers and who dare to accuse the Soviets of carrying on a policy of constraint towards the peasants . . . . The enthusiasm of the peasant masses for collective economics has upset all the earliest plans." My readers will recall my remark about the Communist attitude to the Eighth Commandment. The following objective statement by William Henry Chamberlin ought to convince them of the necessity of bearing it in mind. Mr. Chamberlin, who spent nearly twelve years in the Soviet Union, writes as follows: "The Russian Communists never won the sympathy of the peasants for their program of state-controlled collectivist agriculture. What they did was to ride into power by exploiting the peasants' desire to seize for their own possession, the large estates of the landlords, and then to clamp down such a ruthless dictatorship that the peasants, however much they might squirm and writhe, could never obtain the right to own and farm the land on the individual basis which they desired. The best proof of the peasants' individualist preference lies in the fact that less than 2% of them entered collective farms until extreme state pressure was used to compel them to do so, beginning in 1929."[2]

WHO WAS RESPONSIBLE FOR THE LIQUIDATION OF THE KULAKS?

"On December 27th (1929)," writes Eugene Lyons (op. cit., p. 276), "the press published the text of an address made by Stalin two days earlier (Christmas Day, Feast of the Nativity of Our Lord) to a group of agrarian officials, in which he raised the slogan of 'liquidation of the kulaks as a class.' It was the signal for the most startling piece of brutality, considering its dimensions,

---

[2.] *Collectivism: A False Utopia* (p. 198). Quoted by the kind permission of the MacMillan Company, publishers. This work was published in 1937.

in the annals of revolution. Stalin neither defined a kulak nor cautioned against excesses. Meek Russian historians and their complacent foreign parrots have carefully revised the record of this time to shift the responsibility for the horrors from Stalin to his supposedly 'over-zealous' local agents." This is precisely the line followed in the Communist pamphlet, *Soviet Policy in Agriculture* (pp. 19-22). We read therein: "In presence of the enthusiasm of the peasant masses and the facility with which the agricultural productive co-operatives sprang up, certain organizations of the Party and local Soviets forgot the principles of Communist policy . . .. These 'lefts' instead of applying the policy of the Party, distorted and disfigured it, bringing grist to the anti-Soviet mill . . .. These organizations broke with the principles of Bolshevik policy and employed constraint to create the collective farms, instead of proceeding to the work of propaganda, of persuasion among the peasants."

"No one who was there on December 27th and the months that followed," continues Eugene Lyons, "had the slightest doubt who issued the order or what the order was. What Stalin said and the deliberate vagueness and ambiguity of his use of the word kulak were an unequivocal invitation—more, an imperious command—to smash and disperse between five and ten million peasant men, women and children, as quickly and as rapaciously as possible."

In his book, *I Choose Freedom*, Victor Kravchenko clearly shows that the orders for systematic cruelty came from the Politburo. In Moscow, he went to see Lazarev, a former friend, who now occupied an important post in the Moscow University and served on powerful committees of the Communist Party. Kravchenko had hitherto, as he puts it, "edged away from opportunities to go into the nearby collectivization areas." Lazarev had just returned from the Ukraine, near Odessa, where his job was to put through the collectivization in one region. "He (Lazarev) had gone to Odessa, he told me, as one of a committee of trusted Party people from Moscow, after many of the local leaders had been dismissed for failure to accomplish the tasks set for the area. Peasant resistance there was especially embittered, often suicidal, and the 'firm measures' for dealing with it seemed beyond the capacity of the Odessa officials. The situation was considered so serious that Molotov himself came down, on behalf of the Politburo, to stiffen the government's ruthlessness. 'Comrade Molotov called the activists together,' Lazarev said, 'and he talked plainly, sharply. The job must be done, no matter how many lives it cost, he told us. As long as there were millions of small landowners in the country, he said, the revolution was in danger . . . .. There was no room for softness or regrets.' We did not misunderstand him. After such a warning there could be no limit to horror. Lazarev covered his face with both hands, as if to shut out the gruesome memory."

A little later, Kravchenko, along with a number of other Communist Party men, was mobilized for work in the country. Comrade Hatayevich, a member of the Central Committee, addressed them before their departure. "Comrades," he said, "you are going into the country for a month or six weeks. The Dniepropetrovsk Region has fallen behind. The Party and Comrade Stalin ordered us to complete collectivization by spring, and here are we at the end of summer with the task unfinished. The local village authorities need an injection of Bolshevik iron. That's why we are sending you . . . .. Throw your bourgeois humanitarianism out of the window and act like Bolsheviks worthy of Comrade Stalin. Beat down the kulak agent wherever he raises his head. It's war—it's them or us! The last decayed remnant of capitalist farming must be wiped out at any cost! Secondly, comrades, it is absolutely necessary to fulfill the government's plan for grain delivery. The kulaks and even some middle and "poor" peasants are not giving up their grain . . . .. Your job is to get the grain at any price. Pump it out of them. Wherever it's hidden, in ovens, under beds, in cellars or buried away in backyards. Through you, the Party brigades, the villages must learn the meaning of Bolshevik firmness . . . .. Don't be afraid of taking extreme measures. The Party stands foursquare behind you. Comrade Stalin expects it of you."[3]

[3.] *Op. cit.*, pp. 86, 87, 91, 92. *I Chose Freedom* was published in Great Britain by Robert Hale Ltd., 18 Bedford Square, London, W.C.I.

Who Were The Kulaks?

"The official villain in the [Soviet government's] concentrated attack [on the Russian farmers]," writes Eugene Lyons, "was the kulak, though precisely who he was no one knew for sure. Before the revolution (of 1917), the kulak had been a fairly well defined category in the social structure in the countryside. He was the peasant whose energy, shrewdness and lack of scruples combined to lodge economic power in his hands. He was a moneylender, perhaps owned a mill where he exacted ungodly toll from his neighbors, leased other people's land on one-sided terms. Through hard work, usury and exploitation, he often gathered the lives of the less capable peasants in his fist—the word *kulak* means fist—Foreigners writing about the agrarian phase of the Soviet Revolution too often have accepted the term kulak in this pre-revolutionary sense, sometimes in ignorance, more often with deliberate cynicism. That made it easier to represent what happened from 1929 forward as an indignant revolt of the masses against a small and hateful group of parasites. Soviet propaganda standardized the kulak as a fat-bellied, blood-sucking monster, a sort of human spider luring innocent peasants into his web. This soothes the conscience of those writers or their readers. It has little bearing on the truth."

As a specimen of this unscrupulous propaganda we can take the following from *Soviet Policy in Agriculture:* "The kulak is a peasant drawing his profit from the exploitation of the poor peasants and agricultural workers; he is the natural ally of the international bourgeoisie, and the natural enemy of the Soviet power . . . . The real type of kulak is described by Lenin in the following terms: 'The kulaks are the greatest, the most bestial, the most savage exploiters. These blood-suckers enriched themselves during the war from the misery of the people . . . . They have drunk the blood of the workers; they have grown rich the more the workers in the towns and factories have starved. These vampires . . . have reduced the poor peasants to slavery.' " Eugene Lyons sums up very well the way Communists used the word kulak to suit Marxian 'ideals.' "After the revolution," he writes, "the opprobrious label of kulak was stretched to cover any peasant who employed labor or who owned a little more property than the rest. By 1929 it was converted into a generic term of abuse, with only a tenuous reference to economic possessions. Whoever failed conspicuously to fall into line with the Soviet policies was thereby marked as a kulak. If his property was such as to make the title preposterous, he was called a 'kulak agent' and treated as one anyhow. In the old days there might have been one or two or a dozen kulaks in a village. Under the new dispensation their number rose into the hundreds. Any peasant who was too outspoken in the general dislike of collectivization, taxes, grain deliveries, became a kulak. In the tragic months of forcible collectivization there were scores of villages without a single kulak, in the economic sense, which liquidated four or five percent of their inhabitants as kulaks and kulak agents all the same."

In H. W. Henderson's excellent pamphlet, *Twenty Questions About Russia*[4] there is a quotation about kulaks from *I Was Stalin's Agent*, by W. O. Krivitsky. Krivitsky was chief of Soviet Military Intelligence in Western Europe and a Communist for twenty years. In his book he describes the third-class waiting room at Kursk on an icy-cold morning, when he arrived there on his way to Moscow. "The waiting-room," he writes, "was jammed full of men, women and children, peasants on their way from one prison camp to another. Many of them lay almost naked in the cold room. Others were manifestly dying of typhus fever. Hunger, pain, desolation, or just dumb half-dead submissive suffering, was on every face. While I stood there, hard-faced militiamen of the OGPU began to rouse and herd them out like a herd of cattle, pushing and kicking the stragglers and those too weak to walk."

"This was but one mournful detachment, I know, of the hordes of honest peasant families whom Stalin—calling them kulaks, a name which no longer means much more than victim—had rooted up, transported and destroyed."

"The fact that the establishment of the collectives," writes Dallin, "involved the extermination of part of the peasantry failed to impress Stalin. 'What's bad about it?' he asked. 'Why not employ extraordinary measures against the kulaks if it is all right to arrest hundreds of speculators in the cities and exile them to the Turukhansk region?' The establishment of the

---

[4.] Published by John S. Burns and Sons, Glasgow, at 4d.

kolkhoz system in the course of three or four years and the transformation of Russian peasants into members of collectives constituted the most radical upheaval known in history. Its 'effects were more profound and distressing than the expropriation of the propertied classes in 1918–20. There were, however, instances of resistance to an extent and in forms of which neither Russia nor the outside world has any adequate conception. The Soviet press, of course, did not report them, and the cities heard only fragmentary reports of riots, of their suppression, of mass exile. As a matter of fact there were a great many uprisings embracing whole regions, revolts ruthlessly suppressed by G.P.U. troops. Tanks were let loose upon the peasants, whole villages burned to the ground and even bombed by government planes. The execution of captured rebels was resorted to with the object of intimidating and terrorizing the population, and was therefore of a mass character. But even where uprisings did not take place, the authorities systematically exiled kulaks, that is, better situated peasants, the term being applied also to many of the politically more conscious, more intelligent peasants, apt to express protest. They were exiled to the far north and distant east, chiefly to Siberia. The instructions from Moscow demanded the complete 'liquidation of the kulaks as a class.' These, with their families, numbered in 1928, according to official statistics 5,859,000 human beings. Some day we may learn how many of them were exiled; perhaps all were."

The reaction of the peasantry did not always take the form of uprisings, even more threatening perhaps, was their passive resistance. Under the new policy, the peasants were required to hand over to the collectives their livestock and implements; they preferred, however, to kill the cattle, sell the meat or consume it themselves. In many instances, moreover, they wrecked their own equipment. The number of cattle, which had risen in the 'twenties, fell between 1929 and 1934 from 30.4 million to 19.5, the number of horses from 34.6 million to 15.6 million, etc."[5]

"The Kremlin," writes Eugene Lyons, "prescribed heavy imprisonments and other punishments for the slaughter of cattle. Then it decreed the

---

[5] *The Real Soviet Russia*, pp. 170, 171.

death penalty for the slaughter of cattle . . . . But the animals continued to be destroyed by the hundred thousand all the same. It was this frightful slaughter . . . which more than any other single factor, recalled the Kremlin to its senses. . . .. Bolshevik leaders admitted that it would take a decade under the most propitious conditions to restore livestock to the 1929 level."[6]

The number of animals fell, but the number in the concentration camps grew. "It was on the basis of the new, ever growing mass of so-called kulaks in exile that the system of forced labor was to grow apace."[7]

Testimony of a Kulak

It may be well to supplement the statements of these writers, all well acquainted with every phase of the question, by the testimony of a 'kulak.' The 'kulak' in question, a little girl of ten or eleven named Katya, comes into Victor Kravchenko's book, *I Chose Freedom*. A cousin of his, Natasha, was in a train into which Katya came to beg for bread. "The sight was familiar enough, but something in the child's pitiful eyes touched Natasha to the quick. She brought the waif to our house. 'I suppose it was the temperature,' Natasha had apologized to mother. 'I couldn't bear the thought of the barefoot, half-naked bit of humanity out in the cold on a night like this.' Mother at once decided to let the child remain. Katya began to tell about herself. 'We lived in Pokrovnaya. My father did not want to join the kolkoz. All kinds of people argued with him and beat him, but still he wouldn't go in. They shouted he was a kulak agent.'

"Was your father a kulak?" I asked. "Do you know what a 'kulak agent' means?" 'No, I don't know what these words mean. Our teacher didn't teach them to us. We had a horse, a cow, a heifer, five sheep, some pigs and a barn. That was all. Every night the constable would come and take papa to the village Soviet.

[6.] *Assignment in Utopia* pp. 288, 289.

[7.] *Ibid.* p. 291.

"For a whole week they wouldn't let father sleep, and they beat him with sticks and revolvers till he was black and blue and swollen all over.

"When the last pood of grain had been squeezed out of him, Katya recounted, her father slaughtered a pig. He left a little meat for his family and sold the rest in the city to buy bread. Then he slaughtered the calf. Again, 'they' began to drag him out every night. They told him that killing livestock without permission was a crime. 'Then one morning about a year ago,' Katya went on, 'strangers came to the house. One of them was from the GPU and the Chairman of our Soviet was with him too. Another man wrote in a book everything that was in the house, even the furniture and our clothes and pots and pans. The wagons arrived and all our things were taken away and the remaining animals were driven to the kolkoz.

"We were told to get dressed and take along some bread and salt pork, onions and potatoes, because we were going on a long journey. . . They put us all in the old church. There were many other parents and children from our village, all with bundles and all weeping. There we spent the whole night, praying and crying. In the morning, about thirty families were marched down the road surrounded by militiamen. People on the road made the sign of the cross when they saw us and started crying. At the station there were many other people like us, from other villages. It seemed like thousands. We were all crushed into a store barn. . . . After a while we were let out and driven into cattle cars, long rows of them . . . . As soon as our car was filled up so that there was no room for more, even standing up, it was locked from the outside. We all shrieked and prayed to the Holy Virgin. Then the train started. No one knew where we were going. Some said Siberia but others said no, the far north or even the hot deserts."

Near Kharkov, Katya and her sister were allowed out to get some milk for their baby brother, though the guard said that, "it was against his rules." They got the milk, but when they returned to the station the train had gone. "Katya interrupted herself again to weep for her mother, father, brothers and sister. Most of us in the kitchen were weeping with the child . . . . Katya and her sister, new recruits to the vast army of homeless children, wandered together from village to village. They learned to beg, to forage for food, to 'ride the rails on trains'. . . Then they were separated in a city market place, while being chased by a militiaman, and Katya remained alone in the world.

We learned to love Katya, and she came to feel at home with us. But from time to time, at night we could hear her smothered sobs and 'Where are you, little mother? Where are you, Papochka?'[8]

And all the time, the rulers of Russia slept the calm, untroubled sleep of the friends of the poor and the down-trodden.

Material for Films

Is it not a pity that so few people have heard of the events connected with the introduction of collectivism in Russia? Would not all these incidents make marvelous films? *The Irish Democrat*, ever faithful to Communist phraseology, speaks of all those who favor Communism as Progressives. Those opposed to Communism like the Russian farmers, are Reactionaries. Would it not be wonderful to see the valiant Progressives wiping out the Reactionaries with tanks and planes? What matter if the Reactionaries had scarcely any weapons except the few agricultural implements that had not been confiscated? Would it not be a thrilling sight to behold the heroic Red soldiers mowing down with machine guns the starving 'enemies of the people,' as they tried to cross over the frozen Dniester where it formed the frontier between Russia and Romania? "There were days," writes Eugene Lyons, "when the corpses totaled into hundreds. Soviet soldiers were using machine guns to shoot down peasants trying to escape from the country."

It must always be borne in mind that for Marx, Lenin and Stalin, man, being merely an individual, is completely subject to the collectivity. He is just like a bee in a hive and cannot have a right to private property. The mode of procedure adopted against the Russian farmers was not an accident. It was demanded by the logic of the Marxian system.

[8.] Op. cit., pp. 87, 88, 89, 90.

Chapter Four
First Result of Collectivization: Famine

Evidence of Foreigners Living in Russia

According to Eugene Lyons, in August, 1933, the *New York Times* prefaced an admission of the great famine in Russia (1932–1933) with the following remarkable statement: "Any report of a famine in Russia is today an exaggeration, or malignant propaganda. The food shortage which has affected almost the whole population in the last year and particularly in the grain producing provinces the Ukraine, North Caucasus, the Lower Volga region has, however, caused heavy loss of life." Lyons rightly points out that the distinction between "heavy loss of life through food shortage" and "famine" is very ingenious. The very next day after the (New York) *Times* "half-hearted admission," Lyons continues, "its representative in Berlin, Frederick T. Birchall, talked to a group of foreigners just returned from the famine territory . . . . 'The revelation of what they have seen,' Birchall cabled, 'indicates that the recent estimate of four million deaths due indirectly to malnutrition in agricultural Russia in recent months may be rather an understatement than an exaggeration' . . . . All of us had talked with people just returned from the famine regions. Jack Calder returned from a long tour of Kazakstan with stories to curdle one's blood. Perched on a high stool at the Metropole Bar, we listened to his graphic description of Kazakstan roads lined with stiff corpses like so many logs. Most of us saw the pictures taken by German consular officials in the Ukraine showing scenes of horror reminiscent of the

Volga famine of 1921 . . . . There was no more need for investigation to establish the mere existence of the Russian famine than investigation to establish the existence of the American depression. Inside Russia the matter was not disputed. The famine was accepted as a matter of course in our casual conversation at the hotels and in our homes."[1]

William H. Chamberlin is even more illuminating, for he seems to have visited the Ukraine and the North Caucasus. He writes: "I had the illuminating experience of attending a session of the Soviet Executive Committee, a legislative body consisting of delegates selected from all parts of the country, in December, 1933. During that year, Ukraine, the North Caucasus, and other regions of the Soviet Union had undergone one of the worst famines in Russian history. I had only recently returned from a trip in Ukraine and North Caucasus, where I found overwhelming evidence in the statements, not only of the peasants, but also of the local Soviet officials, that there had been widespread loss of life from hunger and related diseases. The Soviet President, Kalinin, made one curious reference to the famine. He said, referring to a movement in Austria to organize relief: 'Political impostors ask for contributions for the alleged starving of Ukraine. Only degraded disintegrating classes can produce such cynical elements.' And not one delegate from Ukraine where in village after village I obtained the most detailed specific information of outright deaths from hunger, sprang up and gave Kalinin the lie direct."[2]

Evidence of a Russian

Victor Kravchenko not only visited famine stricken areas, but actually worked therein as the authorized representative of the Political Department and the Regional Committee. Here are a few extracts from his pathetic book, *I Chose Freedom*: "The first dividends of collectivization were death. Although not a word about the tragedy appeared in the newspapers, the famine that raged

---

[1.] *Assignment in Utopia*, pp. 573. 574.
[2.] *Russia's Iron Age* by W. H. Chamberlin, p. 88.

throughout Southern Russia and Central Asia was a matter of common knowledge. We denounced as 'anti-Soviet rumors' what we knew as towering fact. Despite harsh police measures to keep the victims at home, Dniepropetrovsk was overrun with starving peasants. Many of them lay listless, too weak even to beg, around railroad stations. Their children were little more than skeletons with swollen bellies. In the past, friends and relatives in the country sent food packages to the urban districts. Now the process was reversed . . .. Because the famine coincided with the triumphant finish of the first *Piatiletka* in four years, the press was hysterical with boasts of 'our achievements.' Yet the deafening propaganda could not quite drown out the groans of the dying.

A. Kravchenko Mobilized for Work in a Collectivized Area

"Everything depended on the new harvest. Would the starving peasantry have the strength and the will to reap and to thresh in the midst of million-fold death? To make sure that the crops would be harvested, to prevent the desperate collective farmers from eating the green shoots, to save the kolkhozes from breaking down under mismanagement, to fight against the enemies of collectivization, special political departments were set up in the villages, manned by trusted Communists, military men, officials, professionals, N.K.V.D. men, students. An army of more than a hundred thousand stalwarts, selected by the Central Committee of the Party, was thus deployed through the collectivized areas, charged with the duty of safeguarding the new harvest. I was among those mobilized. Three hundred of us from various city organizations gathered at the Regional Committee headquarters. The secretary of the committee and one of the foremost Communists of the Ukraine, Comrade Hatayevich, made the principal speech He did not conceal the difficulties we would face in the villages. Again and again he referred to the 'purge' of the Party scheduled for later in the year. The hint was too clear to be missed. Upon our success or failure in the famine regions would depend our political survival. 'Your loyalty to the Party and to Comrade Stalin will be tested and measured by your work in the villages,' he declared ominously. 'There is no room for weakness. This is no job for the squeamish. You'll need strong stomachs and an iron will. The Party will accept no excuses for failure. . ..'

"Armed with a mandate from the Regional Committee, I set out for the Piatikhatsky district in the company of a schoolmate who was also my friend, Yuri. The local officials of that district, we found, were unnerved by what they had lived through. We questioned them about the new crops, but they could talk only of the mass hunger, the typhus epidemics, the reports of cannibalism. Yes, they agreed, we must prepare to reap and to thresh the new grain; but how to get started seemed beyond their paralyzed wills. The police stations and jails were jammed with peasants from surrounding villages, arrested for unauthorized reaping of grain—'sabotage' and 'theft of state property' were the official charges. We arrived at the large village of Petrovo towards evening. An unearthly silence prevailed. 'All the dogs have been eaten, that's why it's so quiet,' the peasant who led us to the Political Department said. 'People don't do much walking, they haven't the strength,' he added."

B. How the People Lived and Died in Petrovo

"Yuri and Kravchenko were billeted for the night in the house of a young peasant woman with two children. The young woman bade them welcome and said: "I'm only sorry I cannot offer you anything. We haven't had a crust of bread in this house for many weeks. I still have a few potatoes but we daren't eat them too fast." Where is your husband?" Kravchenko asked. "I don't know. He was arrested and probably banished. My father and brother were also banished. We have surely been left here to die of hunger." Yuri and Kravchenko then gave her the provisions they had brought with them, to prepare a meal for the children and herself with them. "After she had put the children to sleep, our hostess began to talk. 'I will not tell you about the dead,' she said. 'I'm sure you know. The half dead, the nearly dead are worse. There are hundreds of people in Petrovo bloated with hunger. I don't know how many die every day. Many are so weak that they no longer come out of their houses. A wagon goes around now and then to pick up the corpses. We've eaten everything we could lay hands on—cats, dogs, field mice, birds. When it's light tomorrow you will see the trees have been stripped of their bark, for that too has been eaten.

And the horse manure has been eaten.' I must have looked startled and unbelieving. Yes, the horse manure. We fight over it. Sometimes there are whole grains in it.'"

"The following morning Yuri and I walked through the village. Again we were oppressed by the unnatural silence. Soon we came to an open space, which no doubt was once the market place. Suddenly Yuri gripped my arm until it hurt; for sprawled on the ground were dead men, women and children, thinly covered with dingy straw. I counted seventeen. As we watched, a wagon drove up and two men loaded the corpses on the wagon like cordwood." Later on in the day Kravchenko had a conversation with an employee of the local Political Department, Yasha Gromov. Gromov asked ". . . How many (bodies) were there this morning? Only seventeen? Some days there are more. What can we do but collect the bodies and bury them? You see, the government pumped all the grain out of them last fall. . . . What little they got for their work or managed to hide, they've used up long ago. It's all sad and horrible."

C. Food Exported While People Died of Hunger

Kravchenko went on to the village of Logina, which was to be his headquarters. The following day he made the round of that village and found awful starvation everywhere. He saw that his only chance of saving the harvest was to disregard orders, reap some oats to feed the horses and mow a little barley at the sides of the fields for the population, so as to restore health and strength and enable them to work. In addition, he put the local schoolmaster and some women in charge of the children, to nourish them gradually back to health, as the people could not work, while their children were starving. He also went to the butter-making plant where butter was being packed up and labeled in English for export. "Anger lashed my mind," he continues, "as I drove back to the village. Butter being sent abroad in the midst of the famine! In London, Berlin, Paris, I could see with my mind's eye people eating butter stamped with a Russian trademark 'They must be rich to be able to send out butter,' I could hear them saying. 'Here, friends, is a proof of Socialism in action.' Driving through the fields. I did not hear the lovely Ukrainian songs, . . . The people had forgotten how to sing.

I could hear only the groans of the dying, and the lip-smacking of fat foreigners enjoying our butter."

D. Millions Died but the Government Won the War

Kravchenko managed to get the people strong enough to reap and thresh the corn. But, when the first of the new grain was being delivered to the granary near the railroad station, he made a discovery which made him tremulous with horror. "Stacked in the brick structure," he writes, "were thousands of poods of the previous year's grain collections. These were the state reserves for the district ordered by the government, their very existence hidden from the starving population by officialdom. Hundreds of men, women and children had died of undernourishment in these villages, though grain was hoarded outside their doors! The peasants who were with me when we found the state reserves stared with unbelieving eyes and cursed in anger. I didn't blame them, of course, but I exacted their pledges to say nothing about the matter for fear that the news would undermine harvesting morale. Subsequently I came to know that in many other parts of the country the government hoarded huge reserves while peasants in those very regions died of hunger. Why this was done, only Stalin's Politburo could tell—and it didn't." On the very next page, Comrade Hatayevich explains to him at least implicitly why it was done. "This year," said Hatayevich, "was a test of our Communist strength and their (the peasants) endurance. It took a famine to show them who is master here. It has cost millions of lives, but the collective farm system is here to stay. We've won the war."

E. The Wonders of Collective Farming

Though the collectivized peasants were hungry and weak from a terrible winter and spring, they had reaped and threshed the harvest. What was their share like? "After paying the state for the use of its machines," Kravchenko continues, "after making up the seed fund and delivering the fixed percentages of the total crop to the government, little enough remained. A bit over four and a half pounds of grain per workday per person was the average. The amount was shockingly small, far from enough to feed a family, let alone enable it to buy clothes and other essentials for a year. True they received in addition some sunflower seeds, corn and vegetables. But what could they buy for the product of their labor? The cheapest kind of peasant shoes at that time cost eighty rubles, the simplest cotton dress one hundred rubles. At the official prices which the state paid for grain, the collective farmers were receiving so little for their work that a dress and a pair of shoes represented almost a year's work. Since the same regime was buying the grain and selling the shoes, and in both instances fixing the prices to suit its own convenience, it was in truth a system of multiple exploitation, with the secret police and the Party bureaucrats to enforce the economic heartlessness. Some of the peasants might not be able to write, but all of them understood the injustice only too well. 'Socialism,' they sneered, 'Robbery is a better name for it.'"

F. Anti-Religious Barbarity

To add to the horrors and increase the difficulties Kravchenko had to contend with in getting in the harvest, the following order came through the Political Department: "'In accordance with instructions of the Regional Executive Committee, the church in your village is to be put in order as a storehouse for government grain. This task must be carried out within forty-eight hours and its accomplishment reported.' It was a stupid act; a monkey wrench thrown into the machinery of a crucial harvest. 'But Kolzar (Party Secretary), Belousov (Chairman of the local Soviet), and the others undertook the job with a relish.

They had become antagonists of the population . . .. The local Komsomols did the actual work of stripping the church of its hangings, icons and valuables. The news spread like wildfire through the fields. Scores of peasants dropped their implements and rushed to the village. They cursed and pleaded and wept as they saw their sacred objects removed.

'They've taken everything from us,' I heard one elderly peasant say. 'They've left us nothing. Now they are removing our last comfort. Where shall we christen our children and bury our dead? Where shall we turn for comfort in our sorrows? The scoundrels, the infidels, I was helpless. It took all my own and Ivan Petrovich's efforts and eloquence to restore the rhythm of labor. Just when we thought we had succeeded, a new incident upset everything again. It was on the following Sunday. The secretary of the local Komsomol, a stupid, pimply-faced youth, named Chizh, suddenly appeared on the street, playing a balalaika, his girl friend by his side, and singing popular anti-religious songs. That was a familiar enough scene. What caused the trouble was their attire. Both Chizh and the girl were wearing bright red silk shirts, caught at the waist with gold ropes and silk tassels. The villagers immediately recognized their church hangings. Quickly their indignation flared into a lynching mood. Only the fact that they outran the older peasants and took refuge in the co-operative shop saved the two Komsomols from harm at the hands of an infuriated mob."

THE RULERS OF RUSSIA LIED ABOUT THE FAMINE

In *Revolutionary Socialism in Theory and Practice*, by Arnold Lunn, we find the following quotation: "During the earlier famine of 1 921–22 the Soviet government appealed for assistance, but in the famine of 1932–33 the government stifled any appeal for foreign aid by denying the very fact of the famine and by refusing to foreign journalists the right to travel in the famine regions until it was over. Famine was quite deliberately employed as an instrument of national policy, as the last means of breaking the resistance of the peasantry to the new system where they are divorced from personal ownership of the land."[3]

Eugene Lyons adds that "the first reliable report of the Russian famine was given to the world by an English journalist, Gareth Jones, "who made a secret journey into the Ukraine and walked through the countryside." He then goes on to describe how the chief Censor, Comrade Umansky, got the American press corps to "damn Jones as a liar." Afterwards, "we were summoned to the Press Department one by one and instructed not to venture out of Moscow without submitting a detailed itinerary and having it officially sanctioned . . . . The same department which daily issued denials of the famine now acted to prevent us from seeing the famine with our own eyes.

---

[3] *Collectivism A False Utopia*, by W. H. Chamberlin.

First Result of Collectivization: Famine

Years after the event—when no Russian Communist in his senses any longer concealed the magnitude of the famine—the question whether there had been any famine at all was still being disputed in the outside world.

It is not generally understood that the Soviet government *stopped the publication of vital statistics for the period in question*, although such statistics were published as a matter of course in previous years; otherwise it would be a simple matter to compare the death-rate for the winter and spring of 1932–33 with the normal death-rate."[4]

Lying is Forbidden by Out-of-Date Bougeois Morality

While that famine was decimating the peasantry of the Ukraine and other regions, Stalin delivered a speech to the First All-Union Congress of Collective-Farm Shock Workers, February 19th, 1933. Amongst other things he said: "Some comrades think that the transition to the new path, to the collective farm path, started in our country three years ago. This is only partly true. Of course, the development of collective farms on a mass scale started in our country three years ago. This transition, as we know, was marked by the routing of the kulaks and by a movement among the millions of the poor and middle peasantry to join the collective farms. All this is true."

It was really with the October Revolution that the transition to the new path, to the collective farm path started . . . .. It was only our Soviet Revolution, only our October Revolution that dealt with the question, not of substituting one set of exploiters for another, not of substituting one form of exploitation for another, but of eradicating all exploitation, of eradicating all exploiters, all rich and oppressors, old and new (prolonged applause) . . . .. There are only two paths; either forward and uphill to

---

[4.] For an excellent summary of this question and others see *Twenty Questions About Russia* and *More Questions About Russia* by H. W. Henderson (John S. Burns, Glasgow).

the new collective farm system, or back and downhill to the old feudal capitalist system. There is no third path. The laboring peasants did right to reject the capitalist path and take the path of collective farm development. ... The peasantry has taken the collective-farm path. That is very good .... But what tangible achievements have we gained by following the collective farm path? An achievement of ours is that we have helped millions of poor peasants to join the collective farms, where they have at their disposal the best land and the finest implements of production. It is an achievement of ours that millions of poor peasants who formerly lived in penury have now, in the collective farms, become middle peasants, have attained material security. It is an achievement of ours that we have put a stop to the differentiation of peasants into poor peasants and kulaks; that we have routed the kulaks and helped the poor peasants to become masters of their own labor in the collective farms, to become middle peasants.

And what does this mean? It means that no less than twenty million of the peasant population, no less than twenty million poor peasants, have been rescued from kulak bondage and have attained material security, thanks to the collective farms. This is a great achievement, comrades."[5]

If such a famine, such callousness and such duplicity could be proved against the government of General Franco, what screaming headlines would appear in all the newspapers of the world![6]

[5.] *Problems of Leninism*, by S. Stalin (Foreign Languages Publishing House, Moscow. 1945).

[6.] On page 580 of *Assignment in Utopia*, Eugene Lyons relates that Walter Duranty, an Englishman in the *New York Times* service, after a visit to the famine-stricken areas, gave the most startling estimate of the number of the victims of the famine that he (Lyons) had yet heard. Duranty repeated the same estimate later in the evening at the railway station, just before his departure from Moscow. Yet, in his published articles in the *Times*, there was no mention of those large figures. We are accustomed to the very opposite mode of procedure in the case of Spain, and even to persistence in lying exaggerations.

Chapter Five:
Second Result of Collectivization: An Enormous Crop of Officials

THE CRUSHING BURDEN OF THE NUMBERS OF NON-PRODUCERS

"The Kolkhozes," writes Dallin, "were designed as instruments for the extraction of agricultural products . . .. To gather the grain in the fields under the new system, it is necessary that many thousands of workers first obtain the necessary metal in the mines of the Ukraine or the Urals. Others must dig coal. Still others carry the coal and iron ore on the railroads to huge plants. In these plants thousands of workers make steel and iron. Then other trains carry the metal to plants manufacturing agricultural implements, where additional thousands of workers and engineers manufacture machines, machine parts and repair material. These machines are distributed by rail, water, and trucks across the country into all corners where there are Machine-Tractor Stations. At the same time masses of workers employed in the oil wells of Baku or Grozny dispatch the oil to the refineries. The oil is then transformed into gasoline and sent all over Russia by means of various types of transport. At Machine-Tractor Stations and on Soviet state farms, millions of people are occupied in the operation and maintenance of the machines. Everywhere, in all these mines and plants a large personnel of technicians, bookkeepers, overseers, watchmen, directors, is required, in addition to the thousands of workers directly employed in production for the needs of agriculture. Other requirements include the operation of stores, with their managers and salesmen; houses or barracks for handy men and repair men, carpenters, furniture makers technical schools for training of workers, with their own teachers, directors, guards, and so on. The part played by the collectives as an instrument for the 'extraction of agricultural products is stressed in the minds of the peasants by the enormous apparatus of officialdom functioning in the villages. Neither Russia nor any other country has ever had such a huge swarm of officials According to official statistics there were 384,389 chairmen and vice-chairmen of collectives in 1938, 284,390 bookkeepers and 232,421 chairmen of inspection committees. The whole personnel numbered nearly 1,000,000. In addition, there were 1,530,000 chauffeurs and mechanics employed at tractor stations. The total number of employees paid out of the peasants' labor was about 2,500,000. This, of course, did not include employees outside the economic administrative apparatus in the villages, such as treasury officials, police, teachers, and so on."[1]

Some aspects of Dallin's able summary of how collective farming functions are aptly illustrated in an article by A. Corenc in *The Irish Independent*, November 18th, 1946. This writer gives some interesting quotations from the Soviet press, in which, as everybody knows, everything dealing with government policy is subject to censorship. "Here is a picture of the situation on the Gorky Collective Farm near Stalingrad," he writes, "as given by *Izvestia* on 11th October, 1946: 'Of two hundred and eighty employees, eighty-eight are employed in administration.' Not one of these administrators gathers a single ear of corn."

PRODUCTION SUFFERS FROM LACK OF CO-ORDINATION

That quotation gives some idea of the enormous number of non-producers that burden the budget of a collective farm and reduce the basic ration of 'every producer for the day's work. The following quotation illustrates the lack of co-ordination between the different sections of the "farm workers." *Pravda* of September 23rd, 1946, gives a picturesque

---

[1.] *The Real Soviet Russia*, pp. 172, 102, 103.

Second result of Collectivization: An Enormous Crop of Officials

account of the situation on a collective farm in Western Siberia, a farm bearing the proud name of 'We shall win.' It is a lovely September day, but things are not going well on the 'We shall win' farm. The reaping and threshing machine is immobilized in the farmyard. For two days the machine has been out of action because the chains have perished. Now she can't move because the radiator is leaking. Only this very day has the radiator been returned from the garage. Her chauffeur is working on her for the first time and the garage hands have inspected her only once. The results of this neglect are devastating. The machine just won't work. . . .. It is hardly surprising therefore that over an area of nearly three hundred acres the grain lies on the fields where reaped, without even being stacked . . ... This 'We shall win' is by no means an exception."

"The same issue of *Pravda*—remember that all Russian papers print only official news—said: 'There is still a large quantity of grain to be harvested in the districts of Altai and Krasnoiarsk, in the North and Northwest of Kazakhstan, and in the provinces of Omsk, Tuman, Kirgan, Teheliabinsk and Tomsk.' Moscow was alarmed at the prospect, the Kremlin rushed out decree after decree. The Communist Party sent severe and categorical instructions for the acceleration of the harvest. But all to no purpose. . . Hundreds of thousands, perhaps even millions of tons of grain are going to be irretrievably lost. The fact is that directions from Moscow cannot sensibly modify the methods of work on the collective farms."[2]

[2.] A. Corenc is a well-known French journalist. He is a fluent Russian speaker, I understand, and an authority on Russian life.

Chapter Six:
Third Result of Collectivization: No Increase in Production in spite of Enormous Expense

THE LOT OF THE 'BROAD MASSES' HAS GROWN WORSE

The enormous personnel and apparatus described in the last section turn out "no greater volume of production than the peasants formerly produced almost entirely with their own labor; in general, grain crops which had continuously increased before the revolution, have not shown a substantial increase in the past twenty years . . . . Have the commodities produced become cheaper (in terms of gold or hours of labor)? Research to date has failed to provide an answer. But there is reason to believe that the answer is in the negative. The sweeping mechanization was carried out not because of necessity but because of political considerations. Between 1928 and 1941 Russia was not only industrialized but super-industrialized. Her agricultural economy was not only mechanized but super-mechanized. She was protected from outside competition by a system of super-protectionism. For this reason her population was compelled to make sacrifices that were not merely temporary. Despite the great investments the people did not improve their standard of living. If ever realism in the national economy gains the upper hand, that is, if the needs of the 'common man' begin to dictate policy . . . Russia will inevitably be compelled to re-examine the economic validity of many industrial plants, to curtail the mechanization of agriculture to increase the agricultural population and, in this manner, to expand the amount of commodities available for popular consumption."[1]

W. H. Chamberlin confirms Dallin's statements that there is no advance in economic well-being for "the broad masses" of the Russian people, to use an expression beloved of Communist propagandists. "The Russian people," he writes, 'if one may accept the plain evidence of Soviet statistics, are worse fed than they were two decades ago under Tzarism. ... Although 1935 gave the best harvest since the Revolution, it still fell a little short of the 1913 *per capita* yield of pre-war Russia, which Communist sympathizers like to depict as incredibly backward, if not downright barbarous. Much greater has been the impoverishment of Russian agriculture in livestock, with the corresponding inevitable deterioration in the supply of meat, milk and dairy products. ... Here one has in a nutshell the explanation of the Soviet food prices, which are abnormally high in relation to the earnings of the workers and employees, and also the proof that Russians, by and large, are eating less and worse than before the Revolution .... Some individual groups of the Russian population may have gained at the expense of others. But the national food balance is clearly less favorable than it was before the war (1914–1918) .... The ordeal through which peasants passed between 1929 and 1933, the period of compulsory changing over from individual to collective farming, is without precedent in any other European country. Millions 'perished of outright hunger and the diseases, such as typhoid and influenza, that follow in the wake of hunger, during the great famine of 1932–1933 .... Since the low point of 1933, there has been a turn for the better in Soviet agriculture. The peasants have resigned themselves to the state landlordism of collective farming, just as their ancestors, after futile revolts, resigned themselves to serfdom .... But recovery from the famine level of 1933 can proceed a considerable distance without approaching the very modest pre-war normal level of well-being .... The peasants who rose a little above the general poverty line have been 'liquidated' as kulaks, and the Soviet village today presents an unrelieved picture of drab and dingy poverty. If there is a peasant in the Soviet Union who possesses a

---

[1]. *The Real Soviet Russia* by D. J. Dallin, pp. 103, 104.

motorcar, a telephone in his house or a bathroom with modern sanitation, I failed to meet him during many years of extensive travel in Russia. . . Indeed the economic position of the whole Russian peasantry is that of share-croppers, with an all-powerful state as landlord, telling them what and how much they must plant, how much they must deliver to the towns, how much they may keep, what they shall receive for their labor."[2]

What has been said call be supplemented by the opinions of some who have worked on collective farms. In *The Dark Side of the Moon*, compiled from the testimonies of numerous Poles, we read: "Within the Soviet Union there exist some collective and state farms which are better managed and better exploited than the one described here and than all the others of which the following pages might equally serve as the description. Some travelers from Europe, in fact, have visited such farms. Nevertheless in the mass of material at my disposal, material supplied by those who throughout long weeks, months and years, have actually lived and labored on these state and collective farms, I have actually no evidence confirming their existence."[3] In one of the documents quoted in the same book, the following passage occurs: "As spring advanced we were sent to dig out the agricultural machines which had been left out under snow all winter. Nobody knew where to start looking for them; no note had been made of the places in which they had been left. The same round of meetings with the same talk of programs, transport and seeds, began again; but in practice it all went on in the same hopeless muddle, waste and confusion."[4]

THE STRUGGLE OF THE RUSSIAN FARMERS AGAINST MARX'S PHILOSOPHY CONTINUES

The Soviet government had first intended to apply to the full the Marxian principle of the mere animality of man and allow no private holdings in land. After the famine of 1933, however, the peasants were allowed "from

---

[2.] *Collectivism: A False Utopia,* pp. 86-92.

[3.] Op. cit. p. 140.

[4.] Op. cit. p. 152 Cf. *Liberation- Russian Style*, by Ada Halpern, p. 70 (Marlowe Publishing Co., London).

one quarter to one half of a hectare."⁵ "These small plots furnished, within three or four years, a quarter of the country's agricultural production. Before the outbreak of the war (1937–38) the average member of a kolkhoz put in 47% of his labor hours in the kolkhoz, 33% in his private plot, or away from home, and the rest in his household. Millions of peasants began to avoid working in the collectives. For this reason new repressions were hurled against the individual peasant holdings in 1939. It was discovered that in some districts such holdings had extended to the 'gigantic' size of three hectares, and that in others some peasants employed in collectives had two private holdings while others were selling theirs. Orders were then issued limiting the right to such holdings and the right to keep cattle . . . .. In some districts every peasant was required to work in his collective not less than sixty days a year; in others not less than eighty days . . . .. For the peasantry, the system of collectives meant a return, in many respects to the old order . . . .. To be sure the private landlord was no more; Instead there was the statemaster . . . .. The collectives have been pictured as the most modern achievement of the twentieth century . . . .. But the chief elements have been derived from the hoary past, "Of course Soviet policy has not followed the old track because it deliberately wanted to revive the old Russian customs; on the contrary, the Soviet regime considers its policy extremely progressive. But there is small choice between economic systems, especially in questions involving the interrelationship of state and peasantry. Having repudiated the satanic principle of individual economy, but at the same time being in need of constantly increasing quantities of the peasants' products, the Soviet state rally had no other way than to amalgamate the peasants into great administrative economic units and to make labor compulsory. At the same time it was compelled to reduce the private holdings of each peasant to a minimum, in order not to lose his labor on the big landed estate known as the collective; and the hidden conflict between the state and the members of the collectives has continued uninterruptedly over the issue of the peasants' right to own their holdings and their obligations to work in the collectives."⁶

---

⁵· 1 Hectare=2.471 acres.
⁶· *The Real Soviet Russia,* by D. J. Dallin, pp. 173-177.

No Increase in Production in Spite of Enormous Expense

The usually well-informed Bulletin, *Continental News Service*, July 26th, 1946, comments on the new Five Year Plan as follows: "The new Russian Five Year Plan and recent utterances of Soviet leaders have completely disposed of suggestions that there would be a relaxation of the collective system to meet the desire of the peasant soldiers of the Red Army for more human living conditions after the war, The contrary has happened, and government spokesmen now demand a strengthening of the collective system. The official point of view, based on the old theories of Lenin and Stalin [based in turn on Marx's animal materialism] is that two opposing tendencies, the Socialist tendency of the working class, and the contrary tendency of capitalist peasant economy cannot be reconciled. Soviet propagandists attribute the wartime maintenance of a relatively high rate of production of foodstuffs and raw materials to the system of collectivization, which enabled the authorities to dispose freely of equipment and manpower. It is, of course, true that state ownership of the means of production removes the necessity of obtaining the consent of individual owners—just as the un-free status of the kolkhoz workers allows the government to transfer them at will, in the knowledge that the only opposition they can offer is passive, reflected in decreased output."

The Bulletin then gives the 1950 target figures for agriculture and continues: "The main difficulties in carrying out this bold plan will arise from the shortage of manpower [due to the enormous army] and the very low output of the kolkhoz workers. The authorities are now giving much attention to schemes for raising the output of these workers. Pre-war experience of the results of collectivization does not justify the optimism of those who still maintain its superiority as system of production . . . . The real argument for collectivization in Soviet eyes is not its unproved capacity to increase output but the necessity of the existence of a 'Socialist System' in the countryside, without which, as Stalin said, the maintenance of Soviet power would be unthinkable. The Soviet press is demanding the scrupulous observance of the Stalin Decree on Collectivization. This decree lays down the principles of the system of compulsory collectivization in agriculture, emphasizes the duty of giving up to the state the produce of the kolkhoz, and affirms that 'an increasingly strict adherence to the program of the collectivization of agriculture will bring Russia closer to the type of a classless community and integral Communism." Thus it is hoped to keep the donkey following the carrot dangling before its nose.

A paragraph in *The Weekly Review* of March 6th, 1947, referring to the *Gosplan Report for 1946*, shows that the struggle of the Russian farmers against the Marxian system goes on. It says: "The Soviet statement on food production and industry in Russia is interesting if only from the point of view of the problems of a totalitarian state. If the facts given are true—and there is evidence that they are at all events based on actual events—one is led to the conclusion that 'even the most ruthless methods fail after a certain point to produce the required effects . . . . The collective farms, many of which last year the peasants divided up into private plots, have apparently been brought to heel, but it must have been a considerable undertaking seeing that some eleven million acres had been misappropriated by private holders. But it is one thing to dragoon peasants into conformity with the detested collective system and quite another to produce satisfactory crops under such conditions.

"The truth seems to be that obedience has been exacted at the price of a calamitous loss of food . . . . No doubt the Kremlin will get over these difficulties by liquidation . . . nevertheless the widespread 'ca'canny' of the population does seem to suggest that even ruthlessness is losing its effectiveness as a spur to production."

Conclusion: Collective Farming is a Failure

"Collective farming is maintained in Russia, not because it is a success, but because Marx's logic and the schemes of those who control Russia demand it. "The whole system of collective farming," writes A. Corenc in the article in The Irish Independent already quoted, "has, as a matter of fact, revealed such alarming defects, in particular from the point of view of the overall national food supply, that the government has had to treat the whole problem as a matter of urgency. At the end of September (1946) a special decree was issued from Moscow over the signature of Stalin himself and Zdanov. The decree declared the maintenance of the collective farming system . . . and insisted that the peasants' personal plots should not exceed the small statutory dimensions . . .. On the other side of the picture, the decree promises to increase the basic grain ration and to reduce the number of nonproductive employees to the absolute minimum. It also ordered a return to the system of election of presidents by the farming community as a whole. . . . - This concession means little or nothing to the peasants, who are perfectly well aware that the President will always be the nominee of the Communist Party . . .. One thing is certain—a large proportion of the year's harvest will be lost beyond recovery. But the Soviet government will do its utmost to force the peasants to deliver the whole of the tax in kind even for the areas where the grain has not been harvested or has rotted in the fields. The natural result of this policy must be to reduce yet further the 'day's work grain ration,' and the peasants will have still less interest in working on the collective farms.

Let us take another testimony with regard to the failure of collective farming, this time from the pen of a well-known agriculturalist. In his preface to the English edition of *Ill Fares the Land*, by Carey McWilliams the Earl of Portsmouth writes: "In size and in great fertile plains, the U.S.S.R. is the country in Europe most comparable with the U.S.A. In displacement of the small farms and in machine-mindedness the U.S.S.R. Is also comparable; yet the small farmers and the farm workers of the United Kingdom are reckoned to have a productivity per head five times as great as the farm workers of Russia."[7]

[7.] *Ill Fares the Land* has been published in England by Faber and Faber. It may be well to remark that in *America Preferred* (Oct.1945), Carl H. Mote points out the Communist connections of Carey McWilliams. He says that "McWilliams is not only Treasurer of the Judaeo-Marxist 'Mobilization for Democracy' on the West Coast, but is also Vice–Chairman of George Marshall's Judaeo-Marxist 'National Federation of Constitutional Liberties 'on the East Coast. . .. *The Communist Daily World* (San Francisco) and the *California Jewish Voice* (Los Angeles) both published a long frontpage article by Carey McWilliams on the same day, Friday, September 7th, 1945. It was the same article."

Another Proof That Collectivism is not Popular

From another angle, Dallin shows the unpopularity of Communism with the Russian farmers. "In 1926," he writes, "statistics of a (Communist) Party census showed that Communist peasants engaged solely in agricultural work were almost non-existent. In the whole of the Ukraine there were only 10,240; in Byelorussia, 1,350; and in all Great Russia, 51,000. The beginning of collectivization was marked on the one hand, by the dispatching from the cities of many thousands of Party and Komsomol members for the purpose of setting up the new economic organization, and on the other, by intensified recruiting of Party members in the villages. New state institutions were being set up in the villages, offices with masses of employees, and these were naturally filled, as far as possible, by members of the Party and the Komsomol. As for the collectives, they numbered more than 200,000. Wherever possible, their Chairmen were Communists. This was true also of the Machine-Tractor Stations. For this reason the number of Party members in the villages increased from 404,000 in 1930 to 190,000 in 1934. But this did not at all signify any rush of the peasantry into the Communist organization. On the contrary, Lazar Kaganovich reported to the Party Congress, in 1934 that 'fifty percent of the collectives had no Communists at all.' This complaint was repeated time and again . . . . Immediately before the War, in the spring of 1941, the Official Organ, *Partiinoye Stroitelsvo*, reported that there were only 610,000 Party members in the villages, or 19% entire Party membership. Thus after a quarter of a century [of Bolshevism], about 5% of the urban population belonged to the Party (not counting the Komsomol), while in the villages the ratio was five per 1,000; even this included the administrative apparatus of the state. The peasantry continued to stand aloof. This was the reply of the Russian village to the claim that the kolkhoz peasants had reconciled themselves to the new system."

Saint Thomas and Collective Farming

What we have seen about collective farming may well serve as a confirmation, from contemporary experience, of what St. Thomas Aquinas has written about the need for private ownership. "That men possess property as their own is necessary for human life," writes the Angelic Doctor, "for three reasons. Firstly, because every man is more careful to procure what belongs to himself alone than that which is common to many or to all; since 'each would shirk work and effort and leave to another what concerns the community."

"Secondly, because human affairs are conducted in more orderly fashion if each is given particular charge of something whereas there would be confusion if everyone had to look after everything indiscriminately. Thirdly, because a more peaceful state of human society is assured when each one is contented with his own. Hence it is to be observed that quarrels arise more frequently where there is no division of the thing possessed."[8]

In an excellent thesis presented for the Doctorate in Fribourg University, Father J. Perez Garcia, O.P., sums up St. Thomas' attitude towards the necessity of private property as follows: "To prove that private property is necessary, St. Thomas uses arguments taken from experience. The necessity which follows from the demonstration is not an absolute necessity derived from a principle intrinsic to man, whether material or formal, nor is it a relative necessity in the strict sense, derived from the extrinsic principle of the end in view, implying that without private property things could in no way be either procured or dispensed, but it is a moral necessity, that is to say, the arguments prove the very great *(maxima)* utility of personal ownership, in order that material goods may be procured more carefully and with greater order, and a more peaceful and happier state of society assured. To this moral necessity corresponds the moral impossibility of maintaining human society without private ownership. Moral impossibility is simply another way of expressing an enormous difficulty, which is in fact insuperable as things are, that is, given the conditions of the present state of the human race."[9]

[8.] IIa IIae, Q.66, a.2.

[9.] *De Principiis Functionis Socialis Proprietatis Privatae Apud S. Thomam,* by J. Perez Garcia, OP., p. 77.

Chapter Seven
The Eighth Commandment is not Binding on Communists

No Landlords

At a lecture given in the Mansion House, Dublin, under the auspices of the Irish-Soviet Friendship Society, the lecturer, a Major Hooper, stated that "in Russia no one was allowed to work more than seven hours a day and there were no landlords." According to the Communist paper, *The Irish Democrat* (February, 1946), Major Hooper is a "noted authority on Soviet affairs." The Communist paper does not set forth Major Hooper's claims to be regarded as a 'noted authority.' Even if it did, we know that Communists are not bound by the eighth commandment forbidding lying. To tell the truth or to admit that there is such a thing as a conscience is 'reactionary,' 'bourgeois' and 'unprogressive.' The statement about the landlords was evidently an attempt on the part of this Communist propagandist to stir up memories of the past in Irish minds and thus win sympathy for the Communist landlord state.

To make things clear, it will be well to give a brief account of the holding of land in Russia since 1917 and of the present position. This outline will be taken from the American report, *Communism in Action*.[1] "The collectivization of farming," we read in this report, "was actually the second

---

[1.] House Document No. 754, 79th Congress, 2nd Session (Washington, 1946), pp. 74, 73. 75. 77. The Report was prepared under the direction of Representative Everett M. Dirksen.

agricultural revolution since the overthrow of the Czarist government. Under that government, agricultural land was divided, roughly, into three types of holdings: the estates of the landlords, the Church and the Imperial family; the holdings of independent peasant farmers, owned in fee simple;[2] and communal property owned by the village communities, but farmed individually. . . When the Czarist government collapsed, the peasants seized the land of the great estates, and to some extent of the wealthier peasants . . . . The Bolshevik program had called for the 'nationalization' of the land, that is, ownership and operation of the land by the state. Early policy, however, consisted chiefly in the ratification of the peasant seizures. Some state farms were established, as well as a few collectives, but neither made much headway."

We have seen the first attempt at the application of Marx's principles to agriculture under Lenin, then the uneasy truce, and, finally, the return to the attack under Stalin. The American Report continues: "Heavy taxation, refusal of credit, prohibition of ownership or lease of farm machinery, [and above all, as has been related] compulsory liquidation were amongst the measures used to force the peasants into the collectives . . .. In the Soviet Union, 242,400 collective farms, with an average sown area of 1,198 acres, and 3,961 state farms with an average sown area of 6,651 acres, accounted in 1938 for more than 99% of all land under cultivation. The collective farms are associations of peasants operating under comprehensive government control and include on the average about seventy-five peasant households. The majority of Russian peasants have always lived in villages. The village, therefore, generally constitutes the basis of the collective farm. In some cases a village will contain two or more collectives. The state farms are operated by state appointed managers with hired labor In addition to the collectives and the state farms there were in the late 1930's a million or more individual peasant holdings but these averaged only about two acres

---

[2.] The admirable work accomplished by the Czarist Minister, Stolypine, in replacing the heavy yoke of the communal system of the *mir* by personal ownership of farms, has been set forth by E. Malynskl and Léon de Poncins, in *La Guerre Occulte*, (Pp. 155-158). In *L.'Enigme Communiste*, Léon de Poncins says that if Stolypine had been given the time, the revolution would probably have been prevented in Russia, but he was assassinated by a Jew in 1911.

The Eighth Commandment is Not Binding on Communists

in size and amounted altogether to less than one percent of the total land under cultivation.

"Since the Revolution of 1917 all land in the Soviet Union has been owned by the state. Only in the case of state farms, however, is agricultural land actually cultivated by state agencies. The land holdings of the collectives may be increased but not diminished. By far the larger proportion of the land held by the collectives is collectively farmed. Each member is allotted a small plot, averaging an acre or more for his own use. The member has no title to this plot, nor may he transfer it. What he enjoys is simply the use of the land while a member of the collective. If he leaves the collective, he forfeits his allotment. The entire system of land ownership is in sharp contrast, of course, to our American system of private ownership in fee simple, with the right of transfer and inheritance.'

"Upon entering a collective, the member turns over to it all major farm buildings (except dwelling house), all draft animals, all but a designated amount of livestock, all equipment except small tools, and all fodder and seed. These are henceforth the property of the collective, and the individual member may not, thereafter, acquire property of this description. On the other hand the individual member may own privately a dwelling house (though not the land upon which it is built); such minor buildings as are needed in connection with his allotted plot of land; a limited amount of livestock, and small tools. In general the individual is permitted to own such farm property as is required in tilling the land allotted to him. With some exceptions, not even the collective is permitted to own tractors, combines and other large mechanized equipment. Nearly all farm equipment of this kind is owned by the Machine-Tractor Stations, which are state agencies. These stations, numbering 6,000 altogether, furnish and service farm machinery for the collectives, the latter supplying the operators.'

"Each able-bodied member of a collective is obliged to perform a specified amount of work for the collective. The governing body of the collective determines the amount each year, subject to certain minimum standards prescribed for all collectives. The specified amount of labor to be devoted to the collective is expressed in terms of 'workdays.' A workday is measured not in terms of time, but in terms of the type of work performed

61

and the quality of the performance. Production quotas are established for various kinds of work. The number of workdays credited for one actual day's work may vary from one half to two, depending on the type of work and on the performance in relation to the quota. Skilled work, such as tractor driving, is given a higher valuation than unskilled work . . . . There appears to have been a steady increase in the proportion of working time given to the collective . . . . Work for the collective is carried on in brigades and squads, each of which is given a definite task. The brigade leader allocates work within the brigade, maintains discipline, and is generally responsible for the performance by the brigade of its assigned task.'

"There are, in general, three methods of marketing the produce raised on the collective farms. A stated quantity per hectare or per unit of livestock must be sold to the state at a fixed rate. This 'contribution' is in reality a form of tax, and a relatively low price is set. An equally large or larger proportion goes to the Machine-Tractor Stations as compensation for their services. A second market for collective produce consists of the state industrial enterprises and the co-operatives, with which the collectives make contracts at prices considerably higher than those paid for the 'forced contribution.' A third type of market is the 'free' or relatively free town market.'

"As previously indicated, the government owns the land and the major instruments of production, the tractors and mechanized equipment being leased to the collectives by the Machine-Tractor Stations, which are part of the state administrative organization. The government's influence, however, is not confined to ownership. Direct and important controls are exercised over nearly all phases of agricultural production . . . . Under the Soviet system of economic planning, the collective must adapt its operations to the state plan, and to the specific goals set for it in the plan. Roughly speaking, the state prescribes annually the scope and nature of work for each collective, and sets certain 'control figures' or goals. The collective then prepares a detailed production plan. The plan can make no changes in assignments or methods prescribed by the government. Periodic reports must be made to the government on the percentage of fulfillment of the plan. . . .. In addition, a considerable measure of control, partly official and partly unofficial, is exercised by the government party.'

"We have seen in this country (America) an increasing amount of planned agricultural production since the great agricultural depression of the 1920s. With few exceptions, however, government planning in this country has proceeded with the consent of the farmers. The decision whether or not to adopt the plans proposed has remained largely with the farmers themselves. In the Soviet Union, on the other hand, the government's control figures constitute the master plan to which the collective's operations must be geared."

No Exploitation in Russia

Paragraph four of the Soviet Constitution runs as follows: "The exploitation of man by man has been abolished in the U.S.S.R., because private ownership has been done away with." It is quite true that private ownership has been done away with, but exploitation in every sense is there, and the result is a savagery that has never been surpassed. "The methods of 'exploitation,'" writes D. J. Dallin, "are as old as the world, and the Soviet system has added nothing to hoary experience. These methods are: first, wage labor; second, an un-free peasantry; third, slave labor. What is new in the Soviet system, distinguishing it from capitalism, is the universal application of these methods by the state. There are no slave owners, industrial magnates, or feudal landlords in Russia. But the state is the employer of the workers, as well as the slave owner and the feudal lord. Only the state has the right to use all the historical methods of 'exploitation,' while distributing the product as it sees fit."[3]

According to Marxian philosophy, to work for wages for private owners of property is to suffer exploitation. This is wrong. In the encyclical letter *Quadragesima Anno*, Pope Pius XI points out that "those who hold that the wage contract is essentially unjust . . . are certainly in error. They do a grave injury to our Predecessor, whose encyclical not only admits this contract, but devotes much space to its determination according to the principles of justice." On the other hand, a man may suffer exploitation when working for the state for a wage, if the wage is not just. The justice of the wage is the test. "Every effort must be made," writes

---

3 *The Real Soviet Russia*, (p. 89).

Pope Pius XI, "that fathers of families receive a wage sufficient to meet 'adequately ordinary domestic needs. If in the present state of society this is not always feasible, social justice demands that reforms be introduced without delay which will guarantee every adult workingman just such a wage." [4] Andrew Smith, who went to Russia as a convinced Communist, had three years' experience of a worker's life in Moscow. Here is what he says about the hours of work and about the wages received. "In America the Communists raised the slogan of the six hour day, while in the Soviet Union you have a sixteen and seventeen hour day, if you count the seven hours labor and the ten hours *subotnick* (voluntary labor), which is actually compulsory. Some of the Russian workers actually work in two factories in order to make ends meet. . . . In the United States, the Communists demand free lunches for children. Yet in the Soviet Union, even the lowest paid category of workers, receiving as little as forty rubles a month, must pay a minimum of ten rubles a month for a child's lunch, and this lunch actually consists of dishwater and a piece of black bread. We also fought for the protection of women in industry, in America. Yet, what protection do women have here? They do the roughest, most arduous kind of manual labor and receive the lowest wage scale. So low is the economic status of women in the Soviet Union that many of them are forced to prostitute themselves in order to earn enough for their needs. One of the main Communistic plans in America is the abolition of child labor and yet you have children of tender ages working long hours at heavy labor on the *Sovhozi* (state farms), and the Kolhkozi (collective farms), while here in the city you will find thousands of children on the streets as early as five in the morning speculating (trading) or begging Jurov (the secretary of the Communist Party in the factory) continued: The chief mistake which Comrade Smith makes is to ask us to pay the workers more. If we paid the workers more then we all would starve. We cannot do that. If we paid higher wages and reduced the price of food, we would not have enough to supply all the people. We, as Communists, must eat and live better than the workers. During my first year in the factory ten young workers ranging in age from nineteen to twenty-two were brought up by the *Gay Payoo*

[4.] Encyclical letter, *Quadragesimo Anno*.

(GPU political police) on charges of stealing machine parts. I was selected as one of the twelve judges at the trial. During the trial a young Komsomol, an electrician working in the factory, pleaded for the young men in an eloquent speech in which' he tried to explain that the economic conditions in the Soviet Union were such that the young workers were compelled to steal in order to live. Despite this courageous plea, the ten were sentenced to ten years in the penitentiary. About a month after the trial the young electrician disappeared from the factory, no one knows where . . .. The factories are run by the state for the gain of certain individuals.... Here the workers starve and a small privileged group appropriates the products for itself."[5] Andrew Smith's testimony may be taken as typical of the many that could be adduced as to the existence of savage exploitation of wage earners in the U.S.S.R.

There are from fifteen to twenty millions of wretched slaves in forced labor camps in the U.S.S.R. D. J. Dallin's able work already quoted gives an account of the conditions therein.

Communist propaganda amongst small farmers stresses the fact that the victory of the proletariat will bring with it: (a) liberation from the payment of rent or of a part of the crops (for instance the *metayers* in France, the same arrangements in Italy, etc.) to the owners of large estates; (b) immediate help from the proletarian state for farm work, and so on."[6] We have seen above how the Russian farmers are held in bondage in the

---

[5.] *I Was a Soviet Worker*, passim. On p. 112 the author says: "Although the Soviet Union boasts that it is the land of no unemployment, we witness the strange fact that workers who are employed are engaged in a daily struggle to live on their meager income. I have selected at random typical cases of workers of my acquaintance. A comparison between their expenses and their incomes will show most plainly the nature of their problem. In figuring out the worker's budget, we must keep in mind that there are numerous compulsory deductions from his wages for various state purposes." The whole of chapter twenty-six is given up to examples of workers' incomes and expenses, showing that they had little or nothing left for food or clothing, when their other bills had been paid.

[6.] *Theses and Statutes of the Communist International* in *Blueprint for World Conquest*, p. 134.

collectives. The moment they leave the collective they forfeit even the little plot of land they are allowed to cultivate. The collectives are obliged to furnish high percentages to the state and to the Tractor Stations, even if the members go hungry. When this land belonged to us," said a peasant to Andrew Smith, "you should have seen how nice it was. The crops were growing beautifully in the fields, potatoes the size of melons, vegetables of all kinds, wheat, rye and many other things. Five of our peasants raised more than two thousand people now raise on the Sovkoz. We had no tractors. We had only horse-drawn ploughs."[7]

We have seen that there was an exodus of German colonists from the Volga district in 1929. In 1933, in order to refute German propaganda about the condition of those who remained behind, Andrew Smith and other workers were sent on a special trip of which one of the chief objectives was the German agricultural colony at Dobrinka. They arrived at Dobrinka one bright morning in September. They found the village uninhabited, but near it was a cemetery, an entire field covered with comparatively newly made graves. A German miner, who was a member of Smith's group, questioned the people who were praying and digging graves in the cemetery, and asked why the village was deserted. A middle-aged German farmer said that they did not live in the village any more but in the barracks on the *Sovhozi* and the *Kolhozi*, as they had to work from early morning till late at night. Then he went on to explain that the government collectivized everything and, when they produced in greater abundance, the quota was raised and nothing was left them. The people became sick with typhus and many died. In 1929, a number of families left for Canada and Germany, but they stayed on in the hope that conditions would improve. When later on they wanted to follow those who left in 1929, it was no use. Those who sent letters of appeal to Germany or were suspected of doing so were shot. "It would be better," he concluded, "if they killed us all and be done with it."[8]

The Soviet state retains a large share of the products of its workers, both urban and agricultural, and of its millions of slaves, for the purposes of those who control it, including propaganda abroad and payment of

---

[7.] *I Was a Soviet Worker*, p. 85. Cf. pp. 134, 144. etc.

[8.] *I Was a Soviet Worker*, pp. 156, 57.

its agents engaged in preparing civil war and revolution everywhere. It distributes the rest, but certainly not "to each according to his needs." "The highest class (the government employee class)," writes Dallin, "comprising from twelve to fourteen percent of the population, receives from thirty-one to thirty-five percent of the national income. The share of the workers is about the same, despite the fact that they number almost one quarter of the population. The peasants who comprise over half the population, receive a share less than that allowed to the employee class. The least secure, of course, is the class of forced labor, whose share in the national income is insignificant, although its place in the national economy is extremely important."[9]

Why is the place of forced labor so important in the Soviet Union? In order to understand this point, we must go back to Marxian first principles. As man is merely an animal, the whole product of his labor belongs to the state. The Soviet state has vast requirements because of its plans for world conquest. In addition, having removed the "party maximum" or upper limit of salaries since 1931, the upper class compensates itself largely for its labors. "The incomes of many individuals are estimated in hundreds of thousands of rubles annually."[10] Accordingly, it is all important that there should be a vast number producing as much as possible for as little as possible, for "the lower the consumption, the greater the surplus left to the state . . . . The system of labor introduced in the (forced labor) camps takes into consideration both factors, namely, the need of encouraging the worker's interest by making food allotments conform strictly to his output and the need of making his labor as cheap as possible."[11]

No Conscience In Russia's Rulers

Let us now return to Major Hooper's statement that "there are no landlords in Russia." We have now seen that in Russia there are no slave owners, no industrial magnates and no feudal landlords. Why? Because

---

[9.] *The Real Soviet Russia*, by D, J. Dallin, p. 98.
[10.] op. cit., p. 99.
[11.] op. cit, p. 202.

the Marxian state is the employer of all the workers, the owner of all the millions of slaves and the one landlord with power such as no feudal baron ever exercised. Feudal lords, doubtless, did abuse their powers and go against their consciences, but they had consciences and knew that they would have to render an account to Christ the King of their treatment of human persons. Those who govern in Russia have no conscience.

Chapter Eight:
G. B. Shaw, Philosopher and Enemy of Private Property

G. B. Shaw and Irish Farmers

In a letter to the late James Larkin, who sponsored the motion to confer the freedom of the City of Dublin on him, Mr. G. B. Shaw expressed the hope that Irish farmers "will at last look eastward across Europe and be converted to collective farming by its visible miracles."[1] From what I have written about collective farming in Russia, it is clear that G. B. Shaw's "visible miracles" cannot bear close scrutiny. He made no mention of famines or of Russian farmers looking westwards from concentration camps in Siberia or of the pitiful struggle those who have not been exiled are still carrying on against an inhuman system.

Shaw And Russia

In *Assignment in Utopia*, Eugene Lyons has a couple of excellent pages on Shaw's visit to Russia. The visit must have taken place in 1931, as he says that Shaw, who was born in 1856, celebrated his seventy-fifth birthday while in Moscow. "We wondered at the time," writes Lyons, "that a playwright wise in the tricks of stage effect should be taken in

---

[1.] The letter appeared in *The Irish Press*, February 20th. 1946.

so completely by his hosts and guides. Then we understood that he was not taken in, but was himself collaborating in the deception, with the world at large as the common dupe. The Kremlin was too good an eminence from which to thumb his nose at the conventional capitalist world, and Shaw had evidently decided not to miss the chance. At first, Soviet officialdom was uneasy; the incorrigible oldster might play a few pranks on them.

He might pry into their closets for skeletons of forced labor, *valuta* arrests, concentration camps, or make nasty remarks about the hard-worked and undernourished proletariat. He might demand statistics on political prisoners. But their fears were quickly allayed.

Shaw judged food conditions by the Metropole menu, collectivization by the model farm, the G.P.U. by the model colony at Bolshevo, socialism by the twittering of attendant sycophants . . . .. At the gathering (for his seventy-fifth birthday) Shaw achieved the apex of cynicism. In any other man it might have been ignorance or stupidity; in Shaw it was cold and calculated taunting of the audience. Shaw could not have failed to know that Russia was suffering from acute food shortage. Rations were growing shorter; some foodstuffs had disappeared altogether; scant quotas of milk and butter were reserved for children only . . . . food prices had just been doubled. All the hopes and thoughts of the overwhelming mass of Russians were centered on this fearful shortage. And in face of all this, the rosy-cheeked, self-satisfied foreigner stood on a platform and mocked the Soviet hardships.

"When my friends learned that I was going to Russia," he said, "they loaded me with tinned food of all sorts. They thought Russia was starving. But I threw all their food out of the window in Poland before I reached the Soviet frontier." The vision of good English food thrown away in Poland was mockery of the underfed audience . . .. A tin of English beef would provide a memorable holiday in the home of any of the workers and intellectuals at that gathering, and those tins lay scattered in Poland. Shaw talked at length that night. But his cynical tale of throwing away food was the one memory that remained sharply chiseled into a thousand minds when the celebration dispersed . . ..

G. B. Shaw: Philosopher and Enemy of Private Property

Shaw wrote and spoke extensively on Russia after he got home. His every sentence carried the proof that he had seen nothing and learned nothing in his Soviet visit.

. . . Bernard Shaw made a large contribution toward the building up in the outside world of the myth of a happy, prospering, enthusiastic, socialist Russia."

Eugene Lyons forgets that, for Shaw, Russia is a realization of that abolition of private property in land, for which he has been working since 1884. Russia, too, is the latest manifestation of the Life-Force, so he rejoices and is glad. "Read the preface to *The Simpleton of the Unexpected Isles* writes J. P. Hackett, "and see how a man . . . can allow the Life Force belief to steel his heart and cloud his mind, as he writes to defend Russian terrorism and excuse mass butcheries."[2] "Do not seek the truth [about Russia]," wrote the Archbishop of St. Andrews and Edinburgh, "from those who, for interested reasons of what kind soever, have sought to conceal well established facts, or from those who have allowed themselves to be conducted blindfold through specially selected districts, feasting their imagination the while on dreams of Elysian fields which do not exist in this world, least of all in any territory subject to the tyranny of Moscow."[3]

Let us now sketch briefly Shaw's efforts against private ownership and his whole philosophical background. We shall then understand somewhat better why Shaw and the anti-God monsters of the Kremlin got on so well together.

THE FABIAN SOCIETY

From *The Socialist Network*, written by Mrs. Webster, we learn that George Bernard Shaw has been working against private ownership of land since 1884. "In January of that year," she writes, "the Fabian Society came into existence, under the leadership of Professor Thomas Davidson . . . .. Davidson was quickly superseded by two young men who, a few months

---

[2.] *Shaw, George Versus Bernard*, p. 189.
[3.] *Advent Pastoral*, 1945.

later, entered the movement—a journalist, George Bernard Shaw, and a clerk, Sidney Webb, son of a London hairdresser . . . . It is difficult for the layman to understand the antagonism that has always existed between the Fabian Society and the Social Democratic Federation. Both are fundamentally Marxian in their advocacy of the socialization of land and industry.....It is probable that Fabianism, precisely by its method of middle class permeation, notably in the Civil Service, has done more to accelerate the revolutionary movement than the cruder agitation of the Social Democratic Federation. The program of the Fabian Society is now as follows: 'The Fabian Society consists of Socialists. It therefore aims at the reorganization of society by the emancipation of land and industrial capital from industrial ownership and the vesting of them in the community for the general benefit. In this way only can the natural and acquired advantages of the country be equitably shared by the whole people. The Society accordingly works for the extinction of private property in land' (*What is Socialism?* p. 98).

"A later development of the Fabian Society was the Fabian Research Department, founded in the autumn of 1912 by Mr. and Mrs. Sidney Webb. . . . In the autumn of 1914 G. Bernard Shaw became the Chairman and remained in this post till the end of the war."

THE S.C.R.

In Chapter ten of the same work, Mrs. Webster gives a brief account of some subsidiary Communist organizations. Amongst others she describes the Society for Cultural Relations between the peoples of the British Commonwealth and the Union of Socialist Soviet Republics, known as the S.C.R. This is an intellectual group, organized for the purpose of co-operation with Moscow, and was founded in May, 1924. "Amongst the principal supporters are: H. Baillie Weaver (Theosophical Society), H. N. Brailsford, G. H. D. Cole, J. L. Garvin (Editor of *The Observer*), J. M. Keynes, Bertrand Russell, G. Bernard Shaw, Miss Sybil Thorndike, Mrs. Sidney Webb, H. G. Wells, etc., etc. . . . The offices of this society are at 23 Tavistock Square, and its ostensible mission is to supply information about conditions of life in Russia. Usefulness to Moscow is indicated by the following description: 'The Communist International favors it (the S.C.R.) as a fertile ground for Communist propaganda of the intellectual variety.'"[4]

G. B. SHAW'S CENTRAL IDEA—THE LIFE-FORCE

"They [Shaw and Bergson," writes J. P. Hackett, "seem to have arrived at certain similar points of view independently, and each has brought them to a focus in his own way. Shaw was first in the field, with a multitude of facts and instances, launching his campaign for the new religion, in concrete form, from every angle of human interest. Bergson came later, with close-knit argument . . . and more cautiously put very much the same story into abstract form . . . . Shaw was shy of abstract thought. [The Ultimate Reality] is one formless meaningless thing which is not time or space, but is somehow entangled in them, which has no parts but only potentiality, which has no quality whatever, but is itself meaningless, unceasing Action . . . . It can be pictured dimly . . . as 'an infinity of aimless shooting out.' 'In taking your side, don't trouble about its being the right side—north is no righter or wronger than south—but be sure that it is really yours, and then back it for all you are worth. And never stagnate. Life is a constant becoming, all stages leading to the beginning of others . . . .'

"There is no real right side. That is the essence of his [Shaw's] faith and his preaching. In the Life-Force there is no stable truth. To man in his little day there seems a passing permanence, on which life seems to pause in its course and which he calls truth. To linger on one of these facets, to cling to it, is to become embedded in the past and to petrify. Life moves ever onward, and to move with it is to live . . . . 'Try how wicked you can be; it is precisely the same experiment as trying how good you can be . . . . 'There was one danger, there was one deadly enemy of the Life-Force; there was one intolerable person—the man who said that there were laws prescribed for man. The man who said that there were in the world rules valid at all times and in all places must

---

[4.] At the first performance of Shaw's play, *St. Joan*, in London, on the 26th of March, 1924, Miss Sybil Thorndike played the part of the saint.

be eliminated; he was the enemy of evolutionary advancement, and the institutions that he created on the basis of these rules were prisons for the children of the future. An institution may be good for a time, for one year or for a thousand years, but life moves on, and sooner or later some child is born with a potentiality which conflicts with the rules.

"In Shaw's plays there is only the Life-Force . . . aiming at having the new religion accepted and everything that stands in its way rejected. The teaching is always well wrapped up—actors and audience get what they like—there are plenty of laughs and interesting situations; but these things are only secondary to the main purpose of getting people to revise their views about marriage, punishment, criticism, history, politics and religion; Shaw wanted them to look at things in the Life-Force way instead of in the Christian way; for the progress of the reforms he desired was being barred in all directions, by convictions based on Christian dogma. It is not suggested for a moment that Shaw altogether scorned Christianity. He pointed out that Christ was a Life-Force failure, but he always esteemed certain aspects of Christian teaching . . .. What he objected to was the way in which people held on to the beliefs of A.D. 190 in the year 1900. . .. From *Major Barbara* (1915) to *The Simpleton of the Unexpected Isles* (1935) he has waged a steady campaign against these beliefs."[5]

GOD IN SHAW'S AND BERGSON'S PHILOSOPHY

I have quoted these passages from J. P. Hackett's excellent study of Shaw, because they give a very good description of the central idea in Shaw's mind. We may not speak of it as a philosophy, in the sense of a grasp of order, for precisely in virtue of this central idea Shaw holds that there is in the world neither a natural order instituted by God nor an infinitely higher supernatural order resulting from the communication to created human beings and angels of a participation in God's own inner life in three divine persons. There is, therefore, no program for order promulgated by Christ the King. For Bergson and Shaw the ultimate reality, God, is "a center from

---

[5] *Shaw, George Versus Bernard* (Sheed and Ward. 1937), pp. 34, 141, 144; 162.

which the worlds gush forth like rockets, provided that this 'center' is not considered to be a 'being' or a 'thing' but a continuity of pure becoming."[6] Instead of being **He Who Is**, always identical with himself, God is "a reality which is becoming. . . a continuity of gushing forth."[7] Accordingly, God cannot be conceived without the world emanating from him, and thus the world is an emanation from God. God is becoming in the world. He will be always becoming. He will never, be. Nothing is. Everything is becoming, or rather, becoming or change is the very warp and woof of things. This is the pantheism, condemned in the first proposition of the *Syllabus* of Pope Pius IX, which runs as follows: "There exists no supreme being, perfect in his wisdom and in his providence, and distinct from the universe. God is identical with nature and consequently subject to change. God is evolving in man and in the world, and all things are God and have the very substance of God. God is thus one and the same thing with the world, and accordingly, spirit is identified with matter, necessity with liberty, truth with falsehood, good with evil and justice with injustice."[8]

The ultimate foundation of this form of pantheism is the sensist denial of the principle of identity, attributed in antiquity to Heraclitus. In the name of sense knowledge with its perception of becoming (*fieri*), he denied being (*ens*), and the validity of the principle of contradiction. What is changing is and at the same time is not. Nothing is; everything is becoming. Becoming is the very essence of reality and becoming exists of itself. There is no God, pure act and first cause, infinitely superior to this changing world. There is no more distinction between good and evil than between being and non-being. There is no moral law, for there is no intellectual grasp of the nature of things, as there are no natures of things to be grasped by the intellect.[9]

[6.] *L'Evolution Créatrice* by H, Bergson, p. 270.

[7.] *Ibid.*

[8.] *Denzinger*, No. 1701.

[9.] Cf. *Dieu*, by Père Garrigou-Lagrange, OP., pp. 155-157. Cf. also *Le Sens Commun* (pp. 57-70) by the same author. He there sums up the philosophy of Bergson in the sentence: "The inner nature of things, as Hegel had insisted, is a contradiction realized."

The Vatican Council outlined the process of decay that resulted from the Lutheran and Calvinist revolt against the Divine Plan for order. That decay, the Council points out, has given birth to pantheistic and materialistic philosophies, which undermine the very foundations of society. Shaw's works furnish a striking illustration of the Council's teaching. In the *Dogmatic Constitution of the Catholic Faith*, drawn up by the Council, we read: "No one is ignorant that the heresies proscribed by the Fathers of Trent, by which the divine magisterium of the Church was rejected, and all matters regarding religion were surrendered to the private judgment of each individual, gradually became dissolved into many sects which disagreed and contended with one another until at length not a few lost all faith in Christ . . ..

"Then there arose . . . that doctrine of rationalism or naturalism which opposes itself in every way to the Christian religion as a supernatural institution and works with the utmost zeal in order that, after Christ, our sole Lord and Savior, has been excluded from the minds of men, and from the life and moral acts of nations, the reign of what they call pure reason or nature may be established. And after forsaking and rejecting the Christian religion and denying the true God and his Christ, the minds of many have sunk into the abyss of pantheism, materialism, and atheism, until, denying rational nature itself, and every sound rule of right, they labor to destroy the ultimate foundations of human society."[10]

SHAW AND SAINT JOAN OF ARC

When reading the preface to *St. Joan* and the play itself, one must never forget Shaw's theory of the Life-Force. That is the ultimate explanation of his horrible caricature of the lovely saint, who was sent by God to recall western Europe to its allegiance to Christ the King. The treatment of St. Joan of Arc by this latest Freeman of the City of Dublin is an almost perfect illustration of St. Paul's teaching that "the

---

[10.] The translation used is that found in the volume, *The Centenary of St. Peter and the General Council*, by Cardinal Manning, Longmans).

sensual man perceiveth not these things that are of the spirit of God." (1Cor. 2:14). Shaw's naturalism prevents him from grasping the meaning of the fall from supernatural life and the restoration of that life through membership of Christ's Mystical Body. St. Joan of Arc lived and died as a member of Christ, proclaiming to her last breath our Lord's Program for Order. Of course for Shaw, our Lord is not God become Man, and there is no Divine Program for Order in the world. Every manifestation of the Life-Force—and that is what our Lord Jesus Christ and the Catholic Church are for Shaw tends to become fossilized after a time. There then supervenes a new manifestation of the Life-Force, which ushers in a new epoch. St. Joan of Arc, with her affirmation, according to Shaw, of the supremacy of private judgment, was a forerunner of the protestant upheaval against order. To get her to fit into his thesis, he suppresses her appeal to the pope against the tribunal of Rouen and does not mention the ecclesiastical commission appointed by the King to examine her at Poitiers, before she was accepted. According to Shaw's teaching, the Catholic Church could not approve of this new manifestation of the Life-Force. He therefore suppresses all mention of the examination at Poitiers.[11] He also considers it superfluous to explain how the Life-Force lost St. Joan's love of our Blessed Mother and the saints in the interval between her death and the appearance of Luther, Melanchton, Knox, Calvin and the others.

In an excellent pamphlet, *St. Jeanne D'Arc et la Canonization du Patriotisme*, Father Petitot, O.P., shows that, in proposing St. Joan of Arc to the veneration of the faithful, the Catholic Church has exalted the true patriotism of members of Christ's Mystical Body, battling for the Divine Order under Christ the King. That true patriotism is in opposition both to the false patriotism of those who do not acknowledge the moral law binding on members of Christ in public as well as in private life, and to Communist anti-patriotism which denies all allegiance to native land and aims at the destruction of all that is embodied in the Catholic concept of

---

[11.] With regard, to the anti-Catholic French historians followed by Shaw see *Jeanne D'Arc et sa Mission d'Après Les Documents*, by M. le Chanoine P. H. Dunard (Paris, Beauchesne).

patria. "Workers have no country" is a splendid slogan to enable Judaeo-Masonic schemers to enslave the workers and everybody.

G. B. Shaw, Jonathan Swift, and Irish Patriotism

I am here mainly concerned with G. B. Shaw's naturalism, that is with the opposition of his philosophy to our Lord's Mystical Body, supernatural and supranational. That philosophy is also opposed to the Catholic ideal of native land and to all that is enshrined for us, Irish, in the names of Red Hugh O'Donnell, Rory O'Moore, Owen Roe O'Neill and Patrick Sarsfield. "If the natural law," writes Pope Leo XIII, "enjoins on us to love devotedly and to defend the country in which we had birth, and in which we were brought up, so that every good citizen hesitates not to face death for his native land, very much more is it the urgent duty of Christians to be ever quickened by like feelings towards the Church. For the Church is the holy city of the living God, born of God himself, and by him, built up and established. . . We are bound then to love dearly the country whence we have received the means of enjoyment that this mortal life affords, but we have a much more urgent obligation to love with ardent love, the Church to which we owe the life of the soul, a life that will endure forever .... Moreover if we would judge aright, the supernatural love for the Church and the natural love of our own country proceed from the same eternal principle, since God Himself is their author and originating cause, consequently between the duties they respectively enjoin there can be no conflict."[12]

G. B. Shaw has written the following: "When I say that I am an Irishman, I mean that I was born in Ireland, and that my native language is the English of Swift and not the unspeakable jargon of the mid-nineteenth century London newspapers. My extraction is the extraction of most Englishmen: that is I have no trace in me of the commercially imported North Spanish strain that passes for aboriginal Irish. I am a genuine

---

[12.] Encyclical letter, *Sapientiae Christianae, On the Chief Duties of Christians as Citizens* (1890).

typical Irishman of the Danish, Norman, Cromwellian and (of course) Scotch Invasions."[13] It was with feelings of sadness that some at least of the descendants of the aboriginal Irish heard the news that the writer of the above lines had been made a Freeman of the City of Dublin.

G. B. Shaw's pantheistic materialism is one of the modern naturalistic perversions of order, which have resulted from the heresies proscribed by the Council of Trent. His Communistic affection for Irish farmers is simply the twentieth century version of Swift's patriotism.[14] Swift was nearer the starting point of the process of decay outlined by the Vatican Council. Shaw, however, is somewhat more courteous than Swift to us Irish aborigines, whom his ancestors, so replete with Life-Force and fanatical hatred of papists, failed to exterminate. In the volume on Swift by Leslie Stephen, we read: "He [Swift] felt the place [Dublin] as well as the circumstances of his birth to be a grievance. It gave a plausibility to the offensive imputation that he was of Irish blood. 'I happened,' he said with a bitterness born of later sufferings, 'by a perfect accident to be born here, and thus I am a Teague, or an Irishman, or what people please.' Elsewhere he claims England as properly his own country 'although I happened to be dropped here and was a year old before I left it (Ireland) and to my sorrow did not die before I came back to it.' "In a letter to Pope and Gay of October 15th, 1726, Swift,

---

[13.] *Prefaces by Bernard Shaw*, p. 440, quoted by J. P. Hackett in *Shaw, George Versus Bernard*.

[14.] "No such conflict [as that against property] was perceived whilst society had not yet grown beyond national communities too small and simple to disastrously overtax man's limited political capacity. But we have now reached the stage of international organization. Man's political capacity and magnanimity are clearly beaten by the vastness and complexity of the problems forced on him. And it is at this anxious moment that he finds, when he looks upward for a mightier mind to help, that the heavens are empty. . . .. The practical abrogation of property and marriage as they exist at present will occur without being much noticed." (From *The Revolutionist's Handbook*, by G. B, Shaw). That is bad enough, but there is worse. In the Preface to *The Adventures of a Black Girl*, Shaw blasphemously asserts that our Divine Lord's mind was "shaken by the despair which unsettled the reason of Swift."

speaking of Dublin and Ireland, said that, "a man who had been bred in a coal pit might pass his time in it well enough; but if sent back to it, after a few months in the upper air, he would find content less easy. Swift in fact never became resigned to the 'coal pit,' or to use another of his phrases, the 'wretched, dirty, dog hole and prison,' of which he could only say that it 'was a place good enough to die in.'" In a letter to Pope of 13th July, 1737, written "in the last years of his sanity, he protested indignantly against the confusion between the 'savage old Irish' and the English gentry who, he said, were much better bred, spoke better English, and were more civilized than the inhabitants of many English counties . . . . He hated popery from first to last." With regard to social misery in Ireland, "it is characteristic that Swift came to it as a consequence from the injustice to his own class." "By Ireland, Swift meant in the first place the English in Ireland."[15]

These things need to be emphasized. In the August (1945) issue of the Communist organ *The Irish Democrat*, a writer named John Ireland spoke of Swift as one of the first Irish Nationalists, and alluded to Sarsfield as a feudal reactionary. According to him, Swift was "a worthy ancestor of the internationally-minded patriots who gave Irish Nationalism the form it was to take in its later days—the Tones, Lalors and Connollys." In the September (1945) issue of *The Bell*, p. 5. O'Hegarty, who, to judge by his name, is a descendant of the aboriginal Irish papists, said: "It is true that he (Swift) wrote often very ironically against papists. . . .. But the patriotism which inspired the *Drapier Letters* was an Irish Patriotism."

In the *Sunday Independent* of April 29th, 1945, the same writer had even more emphatically declared: "The principles of Irish Nationalism were first expressed in complete and direct form by Jonathan Swift in the *Drapier Letters*." In my book, *The Mystical Body of Christ and the Reorganization of Society*, I have stressed the point that, just as the concept of member of Christ became blurred and weakened in many minds from the 14th to the 16th century, through the influence of Nominalism, so the same process is now going on with regard to the concept of nationality in Ireland. There

---

[15.] The volume on Swift by Leslie Stephen forms part of the collection. *English Men of Letters*, edited by John Morley and published by Macmillan and Co., Ltd.

is a gulf between Owen Roe O'Neill's concept of nationality and that of Wolfe Tone, for example. For Owen Roe O'Neill, the development of national life is meant not only not to hinder, but to help every member of the nation to live his personal life as a member of Christ according to the one Divine Plan for Order. The Mystical Body of Christ, not the state or nation, is the noblest social entity charged with the supreme interests of the supernatural life of grace. For Wolfe Tone, membership of Christ does not exist; the supreme dignity is that of the citizen of the nation. There is nothing higher than that. For Swift, the supreme dignity belongs to those who follow the deviation from order introduced by Thomas Cromwell, Henry VIII, William Cecil and Queen Elizabeth.

In the article in the *Sunday Independent* of April 29th, 1945, from which I have quoted, P. S. O'Hegarty also said: "The government should remember . . . that it is bound to take into its cognizance as equally entitled to consideration all sects . . ."[16]. In an article in another issue of the same journal on *Tolerance in the National Life*, Mr. O'Hegarty declared: "This is a Christian country, and its Christianity remains . . . Christian in the best sense, undefiled by any of the modern heresies and ideologies which, on plausible pretexts, poison men's minds and supersede the fundamental ideas and practices of Christianity." Now, I presume that even P. S. O'Hegarty will admit that Pope Leo XIII knew more about the fundamental ideas of true Christianity than Jonathan Swift. So let us see what Pope Leo XIII has to say about Mr. O'Hegarty's dictum that all "sects" —evidently for him the Catholic Church is only a sect—are equally entitled to the consideration of the state. In his encyclical letter *on Human Liberty*, Pope Leo XIII writes: "Justice therefore forbids, and reason itself forbids, the state to be godless, or to adopt a line of action which would end in godlessness namely to treat the various religions

---

[16.] The same thesis is expressed in another article in the *Sunday Independent* of March 18th, 1945. This article says that the functions of the President, the Man in the Park," should be discharged by "somebody who will exercise them impartially considering the whole people . . . not any particular religion, class, sect or interest," Of course, every government is bound to exercise distributive justice and respect the personal rights of all its subjects, but that is not Mr. O'Hegarty's thesis.

(as they call them) alike, and to bestow upon them promiscuously equal rights and privileges. Since, then, the profession of some religion is necessary in the state, that religion must be professed which alone is true, and which can be recognized without difficulty, especially in Catholic states, because the marks of truth are, as it were, engraven upon it."

Again in the encyclical letter *On the Christian Constitution of States*, the same Pontiff condemns "the principles and foundations of the new jurisprudence" of the French Revolution of 1789. According to this new jurisprudence, the pope goes on to say: "The state believes that it is not obliged to make public profession of any religion; or to inquire which of the very many religions is the only true one; or to prefer one religion to all the rest; or to show to any form of religion special favor; but on the contrary is bound to grant equal rights to every creed." I fear that Mr. O'Hegarty has, to use his own language above quoted, allowed the modern ideology of the French Revolution to poison his mind.

The patriotism of the *Drapier Letters* extolled by P. S. O'Hegarty is utterly opposed to the true patriotism of St. Joan of Arc, and the Communist glorification of both Swift and Shaw is simply part of the steadily developing attack on the rule of Christ the King in Ireland.

Appendix One

G. B. Shaw Admits That He is a Communist

What precedes had been written for a considerable time when the following item appeared in the *Evening Herald* (Dublin) of February 3, 1948 under the heading, *Shaw Says He's a Communist*. Replying to Mr. Kirschenbaum's question whether he is a member of the British-Soviet Friendship Society, G.B.S. was quoted as saying: 'I subscribe to many such agencies, pro or anti-Russian. I am a Communist, but not a member of the Communist Party. Stalin is a first rate Fabian. I am one of the founders of Fabianism, and as such very friendly to Russia.'

Appendix Two

Further Information About Fabianism

In a well-documented pamphlet entitled *The Planners and Bureaucracy*, by Elizabeth Edwards, published by K.R.P. Publications in 1943, we read: "In 1921 Fabian activities in the educational field culminated in the launching of the London School of Economics.....Among the chief lecturers of the London School of Economics has been Harold Laski, for many years a member of the Executive Committee of the Fabian Society and chairman of its publishing committee, whom Mr. Roosevelt is said frequently to consult.

"It is the members of this institution who have been mainly responsible, either directly or indirectly, for the concoction of the grinding and punitiave taxation which has caused the disastrous state of British land. In active politics members of the Fabian Society have retained the leadership of the Labor Party. A Fabian report stated in 1929, when a Labor government came to power: 'Eight Fabians are members of the Cabinet and fourteen others hold offices in the government without seats in the Cabinet.'

"On November 1. 1930, the *Evening Standard* published the following:

Government by Fabians

"Many Labor members are talking about the dominance in the government of that very academic body, the Fabian Society.... Practically every appointment either to high or low office in the Labor administration has been made from the membership of the Society, the latest examples of which are the new Air Minister, Lord Amulree, and the Solicitor-General, Sir Stafford Cripps. I am told that at least 90%, of the members of the government are on the rolls of the Society, and that, contrary to regulations, so are a good many highly placed civil servants.'

"The New Fabian Research Bureau was set up in 1931, with Mr. Attlee as Chairman, and Mr. G. D. H. Cole as Secretary.

"It was in the same year that Mr. Bernard Shaw was reported by the papers as having said: 'Lenin owed a great deal of his eminence to the fact

83

that in his younger days he studied the works of Sidney Webb . . . . The success of the Russian experiment means that old words like Fabianism and Socialism are all out of date. There is nothing now but Communism.'

In connection with the London School of Economics mentioned in the above extract, it may be well to add that when Lord Haldane "was asked why he persuaded Sir Ernest Cassel, one of the richest men in the world, to settle large sums on the London School of Economics, he replied: 'Our object is to make this institution a place to raise and train the bureaucracy of the future Socialist state' (*Quarterly Review*, January. 1929). It will be noticed that a special education differing from that of the existing schools was necessary. And an inspection of the teaching staff indicates that this was to be inculcated primarily by German or Russian-speaking Jews. It is ludicrous to suppose that Sir Ernest Cassel, a German-speaking Jew, provided large sums in ignorance of their objective." (*The Brief for the Prosecution*, by Major Douglas, pp. 4-5).

Fabian Ambitions

On November 5th, 1946, the *New York Times* reported that, "The present Labor government of Britain celebrated its diamond jubilee by filling the huge Royal Albert Hall with devotees. They listened to speeches from four ministers and heard messages from famous members, including their most famous, George Bernard Shaw. His telegram . . . was: "The only message for the moment is that the Fabian Society, having made Russia a great Fabian state, has now to make Wallace succeed Franklin Roosevelt as President of the United States" . . . Thus we see that the ambitions of this latest Freeman of the City of Dublin for the spread of Communism or Fabianism run exactly counter to the wishes of our Blessed Mother as expressed at Fatima.

Chapter Nine:
Another Innocent Abroad

Dr. Hewlett Johnson, Anglican Dean of Canterbury, lectured in the Mansion House, Dublin, on Nov. 25th, 1946, under the auspices of the Irish Soviet Friendship Society.

In a pamphlet entitled *Act Now! An Appeal to the Mind and Heart of Britain*, published by Gollancz, London, in 1939, Dr. Johnson sums up his ideas of the Russian alternative to the Liberalism and Individualism of Locke as follows:

"Russia is making the experiment of public ownership of all the means of production; abolishing exploitation of man by man she substitutes service to the Community for private profit, as the motive for industry. The Russian Empire owns her own lands mines and factories. She works them to give maximum safety and wellbeing to all. The results are encouraging, though Russia is not yet utopia . . . .. Material benefits show a steep upgrade. Moral benefits steeper still. This should be no cause for wonder, for the Russian principle at least is Christian, and the mode scientific."

Now, the Rev. Hewlett Johnson must surely know that Russia's experiment of public ownership of all the means of production is based upon the philosophy of Karl Marx. In the outline of Marxist philosophy given at the beginning, we saw that human labor is the labor, not of a person, but of an individual, a mere animal belonging completely to the collectivity. Accordingly, private ownership must be eliminated, because it means withholding from society the values created by the labor of an animal belonging completely to society. That doctrine is the denial of what is meant by Christianity. Besides, for Marx, there is no God, no Blessed Trinity, no supernatural life of grace. The second person of the Blessed Trinity could not become man, for, as has just been said, there is no God and no Blessed Trinity. Our Lord Jesus Christ is a mere clod of matter like the rest of us. The Rev. Hewlett Johnson knows little about Russia, but he seems to know nothing at all about real Christianity.

Again, the Rev. Hewlett Johnson says that, "material benefits show a steep upgrade." All the evidence we have adduced from eyewitnesses and serious students is against him. He adds that, "moral benefits" show even a steeper upgrade. For animals there cannot even be question of morality, and we have seen the clear testimonies of Marx and Lenin to the effect that law and morality are bourgeois prejudices. The Rev. Hewlett Johnson can hardly have reflected deeply upon the meaning of the words he uses.

In his Dublin lecture, as reported in the *Irish Press* of Nov. 26th, 1946, the Rev. Hewlett Johnson said that, "In Russia he found more respect for family life than in any other country." What does he mean by family life? For Marxists, there cannot logically be any organization such as we Catholics understand by the family. Men and women are purely material like the other animals. They have sexual intercourse, as natural instinct dictates, but the children born of these unions belong to the Marxian state, as do the animals born on a state farm.

Dr. Johnson also spoke of the relations existing between the Soviet state and the Orthodox Church, and added that "the Patriarch had given him a jeweled crucifix, which he had worn everywhere in Russia." In addition, the Archbishop of Leningrad "had shown him beautifully bound copies of the Bible, and prayer books printed in the country." In my pamphlet, *The Tragedy of James Connolly*, I have explained the sections of the Soviet Constitution dealing with religion.[1] We know that animals cannot have religion. Accordingly, though Marxism may make a truce with religion for a time, for motives of expediency, it can never logically abandon its aim of destroying every vestige of religion. It must combat especially the claim of the Catholic Church, the sole divinely-appointed guardian of the moral law, that that law is binding on states as well as on private

---

[1.] *The Tragedy of James Connolly* is published by The Forum Press, Cork. [Editors note—See 2010 edition from Loreto Publications

persons. The Orthodox Russian Church does not attempt to uphold the moral law and is subservient to the Marxian state. Here, however, I simply want to call attention to the interesting fact mentioned by D. J. Dallin in *The Real Soviet Russia*.[2] About 1942 the Orthodox Church leaders published a book on religion entitled *The Truth About Religion in Russia*. This book sought to prove that religion was free and that, in general, there had never been any persecution of religion in Russia on the part of the government. "It is worth noting," adds Dallin, "that it was printed in the printing office that used to print *The Godless*. Apparently the NKVD division, which had previously directed the anti-religious propaganda, was now directing the pro-religious activity behind the scenes. No doubt the very same persons did both jobs . . . . In order not to compromise the Church with a connection with the NKVD, a separate government Committee on Affairs of the Orthodox Church was set up to act as liaison between the Church and the government. In June, 1944, the Soviet government decided to create an official committee dealing with the affairs of all Churches."

Finally, the Rev. lecturer said "he thought the Soviet Union was absolutely bent on peace." In that statement he flatly contradicts Lenin and Stalin. Here is what Stalin writes in *Leninism*: "The overthrow of the power of the bourgeoisie and the establishment of the power of the proletariat in one country alone does not, *per se*, mean the complete victory of Socialism . . . . For that, the victory of the revolution, if not everywhere, at least in several countries, will be requisite. That is why the fostering of revolution in other countries is incumbent upon the country where the revolution has triumphed. That is why a country in which the revolution has triumphed must not look upon itself as an independent magnitude, but as an auxiliary, as a means for hastening the victory of the proletariat in other lands. Lenin expressed this idea pithily as follows:

"In any country, the victorious revolution must do its utmost to awaken, develop and support the revolution in all other countries.'"[3]

[2.] Pages 65-66.

[3.] Lenin, *Works* (Russian edition, Vol. XV, p. 502).

By revolution is meant the overthrow by force of the existing order and the establishment of a terrorist regime in its place. "The conquest of power by the proletariat does not mean peacefully 'capturing' the ready-made bourgeois state machinery by means of a parliamentary majority. . .. The conquest of power by the proletariat is the violent overthrow of bourgeois power, the destruction of the Capitalist state apparatus (bourgeois armies, police, bureaucratic hierarchy, the judiciary, parliaments, etc.) and substituting in its place new organs of proletarian power, to serve primarily as instruments for the suppression of the exploiters."[4]

[4.] *Program of the Communist International*, Moscow, 1928, quoted from *Blueprint for World Conquest*, p. 186.

Chapter Ten
Communist Plans and Tactics to Bring About Collectivization

COLLECTIVISM IS ALWAYS THE AIM OF MARXISTS

State farming and collective farming will always and everywhere be the ultimate aim of Communists. Marxism will always seek to eliminate private ownership, for private ownership, as we have seen, means withholding from society the values created by the labor of an animal belonging completely to society. "Advocating and propagating the dialectical materialism of Marx and Engels, and employing it as a revolutionary method of conceiving reality, in view of the revolutionary transformation of that reality, the Communist International wages an active struggle against all forms of bourgeois philosophy and against all forms of theoretical and practical opportunism."[1] As human beings are merely animals, the independence of farmers must be done away with. They must be subordinated to the property-less majority in the towns, and both town and country must be made subservient to the aims of those who control Russia.

THE SOURCES OF INFORMATION

How is this to be achieved in practice? An outline of the procedure to be followed by Communist agents and their dupes is to be found in two documents, namely, *Theses and Statutes of the Communist*

---

[1] *Program of the Communist International*, Moscow, 1928, quoted from *Blueprint for World Conquest* p.153.

International, adopted at the Second World Congress, Moscow, 1920, and *The Program of the Communist International* drawn up at the Sixth World Congress, Moscow, 1928.[2]

"None but the city industrial proletariat, led by the Communist Party," we read, "can emancipate the laboring masses in the country from the yoke of capital and landlordism . . . . There is no salvation for the peasants except to join the Communist proletariat. The proletariat becomes a truly revolutionary class, truly Socialist in its actions, only by acting as the vanguard of all those who work and are being exploited . . . and this cannot be achieved without carrying the class struggle into the agricultural districts, without making the laboring masses of the country all gather around the Communist Party of the town proletariat, without the peasants being educated by the town proletariat."[3]

"The dictatorship of the proletariat implies that the industrial workers alone are capable of leading the entire mass of the toilers."[4] Complete subjection to Moscow must be maintained in the Communist ranks. "In order that revolutionary work and revolutionary action may be coordinated and in order that these activities may be guided most successfully, the international proletariat must be bound by international class discipline, for which, first of all, it is most important to have the strictest international discipline in the Communist ranks. This international Communist discipline must find expression in the subordination of the particular and local interests of the movement to its general and lasting interests and in the strict fulfillment by all members, of the decisions passed by the leading bodies of the Communist International."[5]

[2.] These have been published in the work quoted in the previous note. They will be referred to respectively, as *Theses in Blueprint for World Conquest* and *Program in Blueprint for World Conquest*. *Blueprint for World Conquest* is published by Human Events Associates, 608 South Dearborn Street, Chicago 5, U.S.A., and is quoted with the kind permission of the President. I have put certain passages in italic type for emphasis.

[3.] *Theses in Blueprint for World Conquest*, p. 132.

[4.] *Blueprint for World Conquest*, p. 202.

[5.] *Program in Blueprint for World Conquest*, p. 244.

Communist Plans and Tactics for Collectivization

THE COUNTRY GROUPS TO BE EDUCATED AND DUPED

"The laboring and exploited masses in the country, which the town proletariat must lead on to the fight or at least win over to its side, are represented in all capitalist countries by the following groups: (a) In the first place, the agricultural proletariat, the hired laborers (by the year, by the day, by the job), making their living by wage labor in capitalist, agricultural or industrial establishments. The independent organization of this class, separated from the other groups of the country's population . . . and an energetic propaganda among it, in order to win it over to the side of the Soviet power and of the dictatorship of the proletariat—*such is the fundamental task of the Communist Parties in all countries;* (b) In the second place, the semi-proletariat or small peasants, those who make their living, partly by working for wages in agricultural and industrial capitalist establishments, partly by toiling on their own or on a rented parcel of land yielding but a part of the necessary food produce for their families . . . . Provided that the work of the Communist Party is well organized, this group is sure to side with the Communists, the conditions of life of these half-proletarians being very hard, the advantage the Soviet power and the dictatorship of the proletariat would bring them being enormous and immediate . . . . (c) In the third place, the little proprietors, the small farmers who possess by right of ownership or on rent small portions of land which satisfy the needs of their family and of their farming without requiring any additional wage labor. This part of the population as a class gains everything by the victory of the proletariat . . . . At the same time the Communist Party should be thoroughly aware that during the transitional period leading from Capitalism to Communism, i.e., during the dictatorship of the proletariat, at least some partial hesitations are inevitable in this class in favor of unrestricted commerce and free use of the rights of private property. For this class, being a seller of commodities (although on a small scale) is necessarily demoralized by profit-hunting and habits of proprietorship. And yet provided there is a consistent proletarian policy, and the victorious proletariat deals relentlessly with the owners of the large estates and landed peasants, the hesitations of the class in question will not be considerable . . . . All these three groups taken together constitute the majority of the agrarian population in all capitalist countries. This guarantees in full the success of the proletarian revolution, not only in the towns but in the country as well."[6]

Groups to be Duped and Neutralized

"The 'middle peasantry' in the economic sense consists of small landowners who possess, by the right of ownership or rent, portions of land, which, although small, nevertheless may yield under capitalist rule not only a scanty provision for the family and the needs of the farm, but also the possibility of accumulating a certain surplus (which, at least in the best years, could be transformed into capital), and which need to employ wage labor The revolutionary proletariat cannot make it its aim, at least for the nearest future, and for the beginning of the period of the proletarian dictatorship, to win this group over to its side. The proletariat will have to content itself with neutralizing this group, i.e., with making it take a neutral position in the struggle between the proletariat and the bourgeoisie. The vacillation of this group is unavoidable, and in the beginning of the new epoch its predominating tendency in the advanced capitalist countries will be in favor of the bourgeoisie, for the ideas and sentiments of owners of private property are predominant here . . .. *The proletarian state power cannot at once abolish private property in most of the capitalist countries*, but must do away with all duties and levies imposed upon this class of people by the landlords; it will also secure to the small and middle peasantry the ownership of their land holdings, and enlarge them. The combination of such measures together with a relentless struggle against the bourgeoisie guarantees the full success of the neutralization policy. *The transition to collective agriculture must be managed with much circumspection and step by step.*"[7]

[6.] *Theses in Blueprint for World Conquest*, pp. 133–135.

[7.] *Theses in Blueprint for World Conquest*, pp. 136–138.

Group to be Exterminated

"The landed peasants or farmers are capitalists in agriculture, managing their lands usually with several hired laborers. They are connected with the 'peasantry' only by their low standard of culture, their way of living, their personal manual work of their land. This is the most numerous element of the bourgeoisie class, and the decided enemy of the revolutionary proletariat. The chief attention of the Communist Party in the rural districts must be given to the struggle against this element, to the liberation of the laboring and exploited majority of the rural population from the moral and political influence of these exploiters. After the victory of the proletariat in the towns this class will inevitably oppose it by all means. . . . The revolutionary proletariat must, therefore, begin to prepare the necessary force for the disarming of every single man of this class, and together with the overthrow of the capitalists in industry, the proletariat must deal a relentless crushing blow to this class. To that end it must arm the rural proletariat and organize Soviets in the country, with no room for exploiters and a preponderant place reserved to the proletarians and semi-proletarians.

"The struggle against the landed peasants (in the Russian revolution) became very complicated and prolonged owing to a number of special circumstances . . . . As far as these adverse conditions do not exist in the advanced countries, the revolutionary proletariat in Europe and America must prepare with much more energy and carry out a much more rapid and complete victory over the resistance of the landed peasantry, depriving it of all possibility of resistance .... The revolutionary proletariat must proceed to an immediate and unconditional confiscation of the estates of the landowners and big landlords, that is, of all those who systematically employ, wage labor directly or through their tenants, exploiting all the small (and not infrequently also the middle) peasantry in the neighborhood . . . . No propaganda can be permitted in the ranks of the Communist Parties in favor of an indemnity to be paid to the owners of large estates for their expropriation. . . . . In countries where large landholdings are insignificant in number, while a great number of small tenants are in search of land, there the distribution of the large holdings can prove a sure means of winning the peasantry for the revolution.... The first and most important task of the proletarian state is to secure a lasting victory . . .. Only by persuading the middle peasantry to maintain a neutral attitude, and by gaining the support of a large part, if not the whole, of the small peasantry can the lasting maintenance of the proletarian power be secured.

The victory of Socialism over Capitalism will he definitely secured at the time when the proletarian state power, after having finally subdued all resistance of the exploiters and secured for itself a complete and absolute submission, will reorganize the whole industry on the basis of wholesale collective production."[8]

"The complete abolition of private property in land and the nationalization of the land, cannot be brought about immediately in the more developed capitalist countries, where the principle of private property is deep-rooted among broad strata of the peasantry in such countries, the nationalization of all the land can only be brought about gradually, by means of a series of transitional measures."[9]

STRIKES IN RURAL DISTRICTS

We have seen that the bigger landowners are to be attacked first and that the middle and small farmers are to be won over by bribes in the forms of additional portions of land, but all that is mere camouflage. All the land is to be nationalized, and collective farming is to be imposed on all, as soon as the suitable moment has come. To educate the rural proletarians and semi-proletarians for the disorganization of the countryside, the strike weapon must be employed. Here are Moscow's instructions: *"The enormous difficulty of organization and education for the revolutionary struggle of the agrarian laboring masses placed by capitalism in conditions of particular oppression, dispersion and often a mediaeval dependence, require from the Communist Parties a special attention to the strike movement in the rural districts. It requires an enforced support and wide development of mass strikes of the agrarian proletarians and semi-proletarians. The experience of*

[8.] *Theses in Blueprint for World Conquest,* pp. 138–142,

[9.] *Program in Blueprint for World Conquest,* p. 196.

the Russian revolutions of 1905 and 1917, confirmed and enlarged now by the experience of Germany, Poland, Italy, England, and other advanced countries show that only the development of mass strike struggles (under certain conditions the small peasants are also to be drawn into the strikes) will shake the inactivity of the country population, arouse in them a class consciousness of the necessity of class organization in the exploited masses in the country, and show them the obvious practical advantage of their joining the town workers. From this standpoint the promotion of unions of agricultural workers and the co-operation of Communists in the land and lumber workers organizations are of great importance. The Communists must, likewise, support the co-operative organization's formed by the exploited agricultural population closely connected with the revolutionary labor movement. A vigorous agitation is likewise to be carried on among the small peasants . . .. The Communist Parties must make all efforts possible to start, as soon as possible, setting up Soviets in the country, and these Soviets must be chiefly composed of wage-workers and semi-proletarians. *Only by being in close connection with the mass strike trouble of the most oppressed class will the Soviets be able to serve fully their ends and become sufficiently firm to dominate (and later to include in their ranks) the small peasants.*"[10]

"The Communist Party must secure for itself the whole of that stratum of the rural population that stands closest to the proletariat—i.e., the agricultural laborers and the rural poor. To this end the agricultural laborers must be organized in separate organizations; all possible support must be given them in their struggle against the rural bourgeoisie, and strenuous work must be carried on among the small allotment farmers and small peasants."[11]

[10.] *Theses* in *Blueprint for World Conquest*, pp. 143-144.
[11.] *Program* in *Blueprint for World Conquest*, p. 236.

The Preparation of Communist Domination in Colonies and Dependent Countries

'With regard to those states and nationalities where a backward, mainly feudal, patriarchal or patriarchal-agrarian regime prevails, the following must be borne in mind—(1) All Communist Parties must, give active support to the revolutionary movements of liberation, the form of support to be determined by a study of existing conditions, carried on by the Party wherever there is such. This duty of rendering active support is to be imposed, in the first place, on the workers of those countries on whom the subject nation is dependent in a colonial or financial way; (2) *Naturally, a struggle must be carried on against the reactionary mediaeval influences of the clergy, the Christian missions and similar elements* . . .. Foreign domination has obstructed the free development of the social forces therefore its overthrow is the first step towards a revolution in the colonies. Thus, *to help to overthrow the foreign rule in the colonies is not to endorse the nationalist aspirations of the native bourgeoisie, but to open the way to the liberation of the smothered proletariat there.* There are to be found in the dependent countries two distinct movements which every day grow farther apart from each other. One is the bourgeois democratic nationalist movement, with a program of political independence under the bourgeois order, and the other is the mass action of the poor and ignorant peasants and workers for their liberation from all sorts of exploitation. The former endeavor to control the latter, and often succeed to a certain extent, but the Communist International must struggle against such control and help to develop class consciousness in the working masses of the colonies. The first step towards revolution in the colonies must be the overthrow of foreign capitalism. *In its first stages, the revolution in the colonies must be carried on with a program which will include many petty bourgeois reform clauses, such as division of land, etc.* But from this it does not at all follow that the leadership of the revolution will have to be surrendered to the bourgeois democrats. On the contrary, the proletarian parties must carry on vigorous and systematic propaganda of the Soviet ideas, and organize the peasants and workers' Soviets as soon as possible.[12]

[12.] *Theses in Blueprint for World Conquest*, pp. 123-130.

Communists Must Attack Missionaries

The Communist Parties in the imperialist countries must render systematic aid to the colonial revolutionary liberation movement and to the movement of oppressed nationalities generally . . . . The Communist Parties must openly recognize the right of the colonies to separation and their right to carry on propaganda for this separation—*i.e.*, propaganda in favor of the independence of the colonies from the imperialistic state; they must recognize their right of armed defense against imperialism (*i.e.*, the right of rebellion and revolutionary war) and advocate and give active support to this defense by all means in their power. The Communist Parties must adopt this line of policy in regard to all oppressed nations.

They (the Communist Parties in the colonial and semi-colonial countries) must openly advance, conduct propaganda for, and carry out the slogan of agrarian revolution, rouse the broad masses of the peasantry for the overthrow of the landlords, and combat the reactionary and mediaeval influence of the clergy, of the missionaries, and other similar elements. In these countries, the principal task is to organize the workers and the peasantry independently (to establish class Communist Parties or the proletariat, trade unions, peasant leagues and committees, and, in a revolutionary situation, Soviets. etc.) *and to free them from the influence of the national bourgeoisie, with whom temporary agreements may he made only on the condition that they, the bourgeoisie, do not hamper the revolutionary organization of the workers and peasants, and that they carry on a genuine struggle against imperialism.*

When a revolutionary situation is developing, the party advances certain transitional slogans and partial demands corresponding to the concrete situations; *but these demands and slogans must be bent to the revolutionary aim of capturing power and of overthrowing bourgeois capitalist society*. . . The party of the proletariat is confronted with the task of leading the masses to a direct attack upon the bourgeois state. This it does by carrying on propaganda in favor of increasingly radical transitional slogans (for workers' control of industry, for peasant committees, for the seizure of big landed properties, etc.) . . . . and by organizing mass action. Mass action includes: a combination of strikes and demonstrations; a combination of strikes and armed demonstrations; and finally the general strike conjointly with armed insurrection against the state Power of the bourgeoisie."[13]

All these instructions for the establishment of slavery under the domination of those who rule Russia are summed up in a paragraph in the section on *Strategy and Tactics* in the *Program of the Communist International* (Moscow, 1928). The paragraph runs as follows: "In the struggle against Colonial oppression, the Communist Parties in the Colonies must advance partial demands that correspond to the special circumstances prevailing in each country, such as: complete equality for all nations and races; abolition of all privileges for foreigners; the right of association for workers and. peasants; reduction or the working day; prohibition of child labor; prohibition of usury and of all transactions entailing bondage; reduction and abolition of rent; reduction of taxation; refusal to pay taxes, etc. All these partial slogans must be subordinate to the fundamental demands of the Communist Parties such as: complete political national independence and the expulsion of the Imperialists; workers' and peasants' government; the land to the whole people, eight-hour day, etc. The Communist Parties in Imperialist countries, while supporting the struggle proceeding in the Colonies, must carry on a campaign in their own respective countries for the withdrawal of Imperialist troops, conduct propaganda in the army and navy in defense of the oppressed countries fighting for their liberation, to mobilize the masses, to refuse to transport troops and munitions and, in connection with this, to organize strikes and other forms of mass protest."[14]

Breaking it Gently to the Farmers

As an example of Communistic tactics in working for the introduction of collectivization, we may take an article in the Communist organ, *The Irish Democrat*, November, 1947, entitled *A Question of Bread and Butter*. Readers are requested to recall what we have seen about the results of

---

[13.] *Program in Blueprint for World Conquest*, pp. 237-239.
[14.] *Blueprint for World Conquest*, p. 243.

Communist Plans and Tactics for Collectivization

collective farming in Russia. The writer of the article says: "The methods and results of agricultural production in the western world are unsatisfactory . . . . There is no assurance of an adequacy of food. The land is not made use of as it should be: productivity is low, generally speaking, much land lies idle, and those who own the land are not fit to use it as it must be used, if it is to yield the food necessary to support life and human progress. This is so because present methods lack the political and social structure necessary for full production and for full consumption. By its nature, the question of food production is not only agricultural, but is one of fundamental social and economic conditions. Present conditions are now out of date, but the introduction of new methods rouses the hostility of those who make profits from the present system at the expense of the population . . . . The solution lies in the development of the co-operative and collective system so as to draw men (and women) together to use their joint effort and initiative on a voluntary but increasingly advantageous basis. To put life into the country, organizational centers must be established as a network covering the entire area, to act as centers of instruction and explanation in political and social matters affecting agricultural production, and to serve as transport and supply and collection centers, and generally to serve as "nerve" centers inspiring the energy of the countryside.

Those centers should be foci of development, where the cooperating working farmers and those without land, would decide and arrange where and what crops to put in, on which farms, and to draw up timetables as to procedure; this is to be done with the assistance of trained agricultural advisers and accountants. Here, too, decisions would be made as to where to maintain dairy cattle for the supply of milk, to arrange for an organized milk supply in the countryside. . . .to achieve these things, there must, at all points, be the fostering care of a political party, conscious of its social responsibilities.[15]

The writer turns out sentences 'according to plan.' There is no hint of the grim realities of collective farming in Russia nor of the tyranny of the Communist Party, to which no opposition is allowed. Still less is there any allusion to the designs of the planners for whose schemes of enslavement collectivization is an indispensable means.

[15.] I have emphasized this passage.

THE ULTIMATE AIM OF THE MARXIAN REVOLUTION

The ultimate aim towards which collectivization and the whole revolutionary movement are directed is the transformation of human beings into purely material, irreligious, and anti-religious animals. "The mass awakening of Communist consciousness, the cause of Socialism itself, calls for a mass change of human nature, which can be achieved only in the course of the practical movement, in revolution. Hence, revolution is not only necessary, because there is no other way of overthrowing the ruling class, but also because only in the process of revolution is the overthrowing class able to purge itself of the dross of the old society and become capable of creating a new society. . ... In the presence of revolution the proletariat not only changes its own nature but also the nature of other classes, primarily the numerous petty bourgeois strata in town and country and especially the toiling sections of the peasantry: . . . *One of the most important tasks of the cultural revolution affecting the wide masses is the task of systematically and unswervingly combating religion—the opium of the people. The proletariat government must withdraw all state support from the Church, which is the agency of the former ruling class; it must prevent all Church interference in state-organized educational affairs, and ruthlessly suppress the counter-revolutionary activity of the ecclesiastical organizations.* At the same time the proletarian state, while granting liberty of worship and abolishing the privileged position of the formerly dominant religion carries on anti-religious propaganda with all the means at its command, and reconstructs the whole of its educational work on the basis of scientific materialism."[16] We may fittingly conclude this section by paraphrasing the exclamation attributed to Madame Roland before her execution. "Oh, Science! How many crimes are committed in thy name!"

[16.] Program in *Blueprint for World Conquest*, pp. 206, 208.